Journey Deeper

SPIRITUAL DEPTH TAKES US TO A PLACE WE'RE NOT EXPECTING

Scott Reynolds, DMin

CROSSBOOKS
PUBLISHING

CrossBooks™
A Division of LifeWay
One LifeWay Plaza
Nashville, TN 37234
www.crossbooks.com
Phone: 1-866-768-9010

Holman Christian Standard Bible® Copyright © 1999, 2000,
2002, 2003, 2005 by Holman Bible Publishers.
https://store.biblesoft.com/ProductDetails.asp?ProductCode=HolmanChB00256

New American Standard Bible, Updated Edition
https://store.biblesoft.com/ProductDetails.asp?ProductCode=NewAmeriB00031

New International Version
http://www.biblesoft.com/new/products/addons/
discontinued.asp?pendProd=newinterb00378

First published by CrossBooks   07/10/2014

ISBN: 978-1-4627-3778-9 (sc)
ISBN: 978-1-4627-3780-2 (hc)
ISBN: 978-1-4627-3779-6 (e)

Library of Congress Control Number: 2014909824

Printed in the United States of America.

This book is printed on acid-free paper.

Any people depicted in stock imagery provided by Thinkstock are models,
and such images are being used for illustrative purposes only.
Certain stock imagery © Thinkstock.

Contents

To my wife, Lori. Thank you for standing by me as the greatest

physical gift God has ever given me.

To my daughter, Ariel, and my son, Dean.

I hope to model more than teach you the
journey we see in Scripture.

In memory of a great man,

my dad, Bill Reynolds.

And we, who with unveiled faces, all reflect the Lord's glory

are being transformed into his likeness

with ever-increasing glory,

which comes from the Lord, who is the Spirit.

1 Corinthians 3:18 (NIV)

Endorsements of Journey Deeper

"Great leaders are never content with the status quo. They always want to go deeper – deeper in their relationship with Jesus and deeper in their commitment to serve his people. My friend, Scott Reynolds, not only exemplifies this essential quality of leadership, he also does a great job explaining what it really means in these pages. What he has to say may surprise you."

Nelson Searcy, Lead Pastor, The Journey Church and Founder, www.ChurchLeaderInsights.com

•◆•

"God never intended for us to live in the shallow end of the pool. Scott Reynolds has been a mentor who has pushed me into the deep end before I was even ready. But I am so grateful he did. And if you read this amazing work, you will be grateful as well!"

Clay Scroggins, Lead Pastor, Browns Bridge Church

•◆•

Journey Deeper is a much needed resource that will move you into a deeper relationship with God. In it Scott Reynolds reveals a step by step biblical process for advancing your spiritual growth. I read every word of it and so should you.

Steve Reynolds, Lead Pastor, Capital Baptist Church, Author, *Bod4God* and *Get Off The Couch*

•◆•

"My pastor, my brother, and my friend, Scott Reynolds, unpacks the truths found in Peter's second epistle (vv 4-8) with the gentleness of a shepherd and the bold love of a pastor. In this book you will find the truth that Scott pointed me to in my life 20 years ago - our salvation isn't a momentary experience aimed at missing hell, but a pursuit to follow Christ, to be more like him, and to proclaim His glory to the ends of the earth."

Herbie Newell, President of Lifeline Children's Services

• ◆ •

"I am delighted to endorse this new book authored by my friend, Scott Reynolds. Actually, Scott serves as a guide for us in a Journey Deeper with our Lord. He takes Biblical principles and makes practical application of them for us. You will experience fresh insight into what it means to be a devoted follower of Christ. Read his book and take the journey. Your life will be enriched."

Dr. Rick Lance, Executive Director of the Alabama State Board of Missions

• ◆ •

"If your desire as a believer is to have a deeper relationship with Jesus, this is a must read"

Lex Luger, former WWE Superstar and Christian Evangelist

• ◆ •

I have known Scott for over 20 years as a leader, boss, fellow minister and as a friend. The one constant I have experienced with Scott is that he is not satisfied, in a good way. His desire to grow in his relationship with Jesus Christ and to lead others to do the same drives him. This desire that is in him is fleshed out in Journey Deeper. Our relationship with God does not have a finish line on this earth. It is a journey. A journey that Scott helps us realize and navigate.

Troy Fountain, Lead Pastor, Wiregrass Church

Acknowledgments

I want to thank God for the legacy of my family. I almost threw away the gift of being raised in a home dedicated to the glory of God. Generations of my family have loved the Lord and have provided the foundation for my own spiritual journey. Thank you, Bill and Barbara (Dad and Mom), for never giving up, even when it might have been time.

I also want to thank the faith family of North River Church for loving my family as much as I love yours. God has placed a variety of people together for a common purpose, and I know God is going to continue transforming the world through your faithfulness. Every day I look forward to doing the ministry God has given us. Thank you, Butch Roshto, Mark Patterson, Katie Jones, Nate Herren, Bryan Geer, Jamin Carter, Mike Shaw, Rachel Whitehurst, and Sara Shipp for being amazing partners in ministry. I would not have had time to get these words out of my head and onto paper without your commitment to the ministry and vision of our church. Thank you to the elders and your families for putting in the time to lead our faith family and model for the journey described in these pages. I personally need to say a big "thank you" to Sammie Jo Barstow, Chip Riley, and Chris Shelby for helping me get my thoughts out correctly.

Let me also thank you for picking up this book. By doing so, you are curious about the journey to a deeper faith and a more passionate obedience to our Savior. I look forward to hearing about what God does in your own personal journey. Prepare yourself for the journey deeper.

Premise
I'm All In
going
Deeper

Growing up in Florida, I played beach volleyball, went deep-sea fishing, learned how to surf (when we had waves), and did everything you'd expect from a teenage beach bum. Except scuba diving. That required more money than my dad was willing to provide for my activities based on my academic performance.

My two best friends growing up were brothers, Todd and Andy Mignerey. Todd was my age, and Andy was two years behind us in school; the three of us did everything together. Their family members were all avid scuba divers, and because I couldn't dive, I had to man the boat. Of course, being on a boat in the middle of the gulf is still not a bad way to spend an afternoon, but I really wanted to learn how to dive.

High school came and went, as well as my first semester at college. When registering for my second semester, I saw that my university offered scuba as a physical education elective. I signed up immediately, hoping my father would not notice until I had already started the class. Sadly, the four-hundred-dollar additional student fee gave me away. Still, Dad thought it might be my only A, so he agreed to pay for the course. I could hardly believe that after so many years, I was going to finally get to dive! The class began, and unfortunately for me, the majority of our time at first was not spent in the water but was spent in the classroom where I had to learn about equipment and how to overcome physical challenges in the water to maintain my safety. I quickly discovered that scuba diving included lessons in math and science, like the atmospheric changes that occur in deep water. These seemingly grueling lessons in the classroom are what ultimately helped me understand a lot about scuba and my faith.

Over the years of diving and pastoring, I have heard the same phrase in both circles: "I want to go deeper." Divers always want to push the limits and go a little deeper, to explore different reefs and wrecks found in the deeper waters. A diver knows that "going deeper" means hunting these underwater treasures while facing greater pressure at the same time. The deeper the dive, the greater the pressure. Let me help you understand pressure. When you take a beach ball on the surface and submerge it down to one hundred feet, it will decrease to one-fourth its size. Pure physics reveals that the deeper a diver descends, the greater pressure a diver feels. When diving, you know that your entire body is about to experience something unordinary. Let's take our same beach ball but deflate it. If we take it down one hundred feet, inflate it to regular size, and begin ascending with it back to the surface, we will have an explosion before we reach the top. New divers are shocked by the effects of pressure, but experienced divers expect to encounter greater pressure as they go deeper and prepare for the extreme conditions.

In the same way, followers of Christ use identical language to that of scuba divers and find themselves constantly saying, "I want to go deeper." Often, when Christians use this phrase, they have little understanding of what it actually means. They equate "going deeper" with learning big words like *sanctification* and *dispensation*. They fail to understand that going deeper is not something you learn, but something you become. It's active and intentional. Because a diver knows the physics behind their recreation, they expect pressure as they descend. But oftentimes as Christians, we forget that there will be greater pressure as we dive deeper in our faith journey.

Many times as Christ followers, we can fail to understand how to attain spiritual depth. We equate growing in our faith with merely learning religious lessons. Truthfully, *if the church never learned another new piece of truth about God but focused on living out what it already knew to be true, we'd see unquenchable revival.* You see, going deeper is not so much about attaining information as it is about taking steps towards transforming into the image of Christ. The deeper you dive into your faith, just like in scuba diving, the greater the pressure you're going to experience around you.

—————

If the church never learned another new piece of truth about God but focused on living out what it already knew to be true, we'd see unquenchable revival.

—————

So, I want us to work together through these pages to meet the challenge of discovering a more scriptural view of what it means to go deeper in our faith. Individually, and collectively as a society, most of us are competitive and goal oriented. We want to succeed at everything in which we invest our lives, our time, and our resources. People don't want to waste time participating in activities with no measureable goals. At work, we invest in a product or service that has a tangible measure of success. Socially, in our hobbies or sports, we simply cannot play without a goal or score. It is sad to say, however, that for a significant number of Christ followers, their faith is the one area in life where many have lost the need to succeed. The bride of Christ (the church), generally speaking, has little desire to succeed at becoming conformed to the image of Christ. We have become content going to church and have little or no desire to pay the price needed to succeed at being the church. I'm guilty of it. I played at my faith while going to church for a good part of my ministry and encouraged people to go to church, but in these pages, I hope you find the challenge of Scripture for every Christ follower to be the church.

Paul challenged the church in Corinth when he stated,

Do you not know that in a race all the runners run, but only one gets the prize? Run in such a way as to get the prize. Everyone who competes in the games goes into strict training. They do it to get a crown that will not last; but **we do it** [go into strict spiritual training] to get a crown that will last forever. Therefore I do not run like a man running aimlessly; I do not fight like a man beating the air.

—1 Corinthians 9:24–26 (NIV, emphasis by author)

You see, being lazy is easy. I know that laziness comes naturally to many of us, but we will not succeed without regular, regimented training and a willingness to go deeper. When I coached my children's sports teams, I listened to players tell me all kinds of excuses for not wanting to practice and train. They never had time to train on their own, and practice was long and hot. They didn't see the point in many of the drills we ran. Excuses and more excuses! Every single player faced a choice, and the athletes who stuck with the plan, did the work, and overcame the inclination to be lazy saw results in their game. The apostle Paul frequently used sports illustrations and wanted the church to see results in their game. He knew that Scripture had the goal of seeing them move toward the image of Christ.

"For those He foreknew He also predestined to be conformed to the image of His Son, so that He would be the firstborn among many brothers" (Romans 8:29 HCSB).

You may think to yourself, "But I thought salvation was the goal and heaven was the prize? If I'm saved, what's the push for a life conformed to the image of Christ? Isn't heaven enough? If salvation is by God's grace alone through our faith in Jesus Christ, isn't all of this extra? Is any of it necessary?" What we must understand and totally commit to is that God never stopped our spiritual journeys at salvation.

Salvation is the starting point of faith-not the finish line! Christ followers have a greater prize than heaven. Paul is not speaking about heaven; he's talking about a greater pursuit. Heaven is not our goal- heaven is the place where we will receive the goal or prize of our salvation. The prize of salvation is the presence of God. We tend to believe the goal of our faith is to avoid hell. The modern spiritualistic mindset believes that going to heaven is good—it's certainly better than hell—but it's not worth getting excited about. Getting to heaven, seeing lost relatives, and avoiding hell are not the true reasons for faith and salvation. We have lost the true prize of our faith, which is to one day stand in the full presence of God. Every one of us lost that opportunity in the Original Sin of Adam and Eve, and only in Christ do we regain the opportunity to stand eternally in the full presence of God. Heaven would be nothing without the presence of God!

Salvation is the starting point of faith-not the finish line!

Here is the even more amazing part. God loves us far too much to leave us separated from Him. He is calling us into a relationship with Him, and if you've never learned about God's love for you, I encourage you to mark your place here and flip to appendix A to learn just how much God loves you. Paul knew what God wanted from their relationship. He understood that we are not called to love God the way we want to love Him, but we are called to love God the way He wants to be loved. Jesus clearly communicated God's heart about our relationship with Him. We do not have to wonder what God wants, nor do we have the right or ability to try to change His mind. Jesus clearly stated, "If you love Me, you will keep My commandments" (John 14:15 NASB).

In our human relationships, we frequently wonder how to show love. Early in my marriage, I kept trying to love my wife in the same ways I wanted to be loved. It never once dawned on me that we needed different things from marriage and received love differently. I worked all day in a church, so when I came home, the last thing

I wanted to do was revisit my day. I needed to hear something affirming, and then I wanted some space to deprogram from being around church people all day.

My wife Lori, however, was a stay-at-home mom and preferred to receive love through time and communication. When we were newlyweds and before we had children, she was alone a lot. Then after the children were born, of course, she was spending her days taking care of them. What she needed from me was adult conversation and some kind of activity that didn't involve a big purple dinosaur. I didn't understand her needs, and I didn't understand that she received love, and was asking for love, in a way that was different from what I needed. God is clear in the way He receives our love. We don't get to decide how we are going to show Him love. He doesn't want flowers, candies, or even sweet promises. He says that if we love Him, we will obey Him. (If only marriage could be that clear, right?)

In Paul's letter to the church in Philippi, Paul said that anything in his former life that was important became "rubbish, that I may gain Christ and be found in him" (Philippians 3:8 NIV). In that same passage, he declared that anything in his former life that was "profit," he now considered "loss compared to the surpassing greatness of knowing Christ Jesus my Lord" (Philippians 3:7,9 NIV). Remember that when Paul wrote those words, he had already met Jesus and was saved. Paul's words are about something he had not yet obtained. The goal he was straining toward was not his salvation but a life completely conformed to the image of Christ.

Paul was working toward the same thing we are all called to pursue: transformation into the likeness of Christ.

> And we, who with unveiled faces all reflect the Lord's glory, **are being transformed into his likeness with everincreasing glory**, which comes from the Lord, who is the Spirit.
> —2 Corinthians 3:18 (NIV; emphasis by author)

So what does Christ look like? The real question is this: does God give us a picture of the image of Christ? He definitely does! I love the description given in Galatians 5:22–26.

> But the fruit of the Spirit is love, joy, peace, patience, kindness, goodness, faith, gentleness, self-control. Against such things there is no law. Now those who belong to Christ Jesus have crucified the flesh with its passions and desires. If we live by the Spirit, we must also follow the Spirit. We must not become conceited, provoking one another, envying one another.
> —Galatians 5:22–26 (HCSB)

Growing and cultivating the fruit of the Spirit contained in those verses is a lifetime assignment; however, we are going to focus on one amazing passage in 2 Peter. In these verses, we are going to discover a foundation strong enough to launch a personal pursuit of the image of Christ. I encourage you to read these verses slowly and meditatively. Let God's Spirit speak to you as you read. This passage will be the basis for everything we discuss in our study on conforming to the image of Christ.

> For by these He has granted to us His precious and magnificent promises, so that by them you may become partakers of the divine nature, having escaped the corruption that is in the world by lust. Now for this very reason also, applying all diligence, in your faith supply moral excellence, and in your moral excellence, knowledge, and in your knowledge, self-control, and in your self-control, perseverance, and in your perseverance, godliness, and in your godliness, brotherly kindness, and in your brotherly kindness, love. For if these qualities are yours and are increasing, they render you neither useless nor unfruitful in the true knowledge of our Lord Jesus Christ.
> —2 Peter 1:4–8 (NASU)

I pray that as you read, you sense the amazing power in Peter's words in our focal passage. He begins, not with a challenge, but with a promise: *For by these He has granted to us His precious and magnificent promises* (v. 4).

What promises? Promises like these:

- "I am the door; if anyone enters through Me, he will be saved" (John 10:9 NASU).

- "But the one who endures to the end, he will be saved" (Matthew 24:13 NASU).

- "If we endure, we will also reign with Him" (2 Timothy 2:12 NASU).

God's promises are the driving hope for those who have chosen a life in Christ. Hope in the power of our Creator is a powerful force in those who have decided to make the image of Christ their life's foundational goal. This goal is poles apart from the secular world, but it is the God-given goal for all those who have become partakers of the divine nature. Paul explains that we are striving forward "so that by them [the promises of God] you may become partakers of the divine nature, having escaped the corruption that is in the world by lust" (2 Peter 1:4b NASU).

Striving to maintain a life pursuit greater than our own salvation says, "I understand what I've been saved from, I'm beginning to grasp what I've been saved to, and I'm committed to what I've been saved for—transformation into the image of Christ for the glory of God." I pray that in the pages of this book, you will be able to hold onto this amazing truth about the calling of your salvation. God didn't call you only to salvation; He called you to be conformed to the image of Christ. Salvation is the first step in that greater journey, and you definitely cannot be conformed to the image of Christ without salvation.

So what is the great nugget of truth we need to remember as

we begin to examine this journey toward being conformed to the image of Christ?

Salvation is not the finish line; it's merely the starting point!

Study Questions

Intro video for group study can be found at
www.myjourneydeeper.com

1. What do you mean when you say, "I want to go deeper in my walk with Christ"?

2. What does salvation look like?

3. What changes in our relationship with Jesus once we realize that salvation is the starting point and not the finish line?

4. What does transforming into the image of Christ involve for each follower of Jesus?

5. What did you learn from this chapter, and how can you apply it to your life?

6. What areas do you need to pray about or improve in your walk with Jesus?

Chapter 1
Will We Ever Get to the Good Stuff?
in your faith
Applying All Diligence

Training to dive was a lot different from what I had imagined. I couldn't understand why we were spending so much time in the classroom. I didn't want a bunch of information, and I didn't care at all about the science behind diving. I wanted to dive. The Mignereys had made it all look so simple and exciting. All those hours on the boat watching them go down and come back up was all I could think about while I was sitting in a classroom and learning about oxygen and atmospheres. I was afraid the misery of class work would never end. Finally, after weeks of classroom assignments filled with charts and calculations, our instructor told us to plan for getting wet the next day.

I was so excited thinking about all the stuff that we were going to do in the water; however, I was bummed to find out that the first lesson in the water was a swimming test. I couldn't believe it, all this buildup for a swimming test! I was starting to think I'd been sold a false bill of goods when it came to getting ready to dive. Session number two in the water wasn't any better. We spent much of the lesson learning how to tread water and float for long periods of time. Try floating for five minutes and see if you don't go crazy thinking of a hundred things you could be doing instead. Or try treading water for fifteen minutes as a part of a safety evaluation and see if you think the certification is worth the pain. I was dying physically and going out of my mind mentally. I wanted to learn about *diving*. All we seemed to be doing was working on safety measures.

One of our next lessons centered on swimming the length of the pool. We were instructed to take a deep breath at the halfway point and swim the rest of the way underwater to find our mask on the bottom of the pool. Then we had to put the masks on and breathe through our noses to clear the water out of our masks. These sessions were a nightmare. Safety, safety, safety. All we did in class was prepare for trouble. We never seemed to talk about the great adventures found in diving. All we talked about was what would happen if you lost your mask underwater or what to do if you ran out of air on the bottom. The most exciting lesson was the day we sat in three feet of water for ten minutes and got comfortable breathing air through a regulator. My instructor was not talking about diving the same way Todd and Andy talked about diving.

Once I started diving, however, I realized why. Friends were selling the adventure, while my instructor was trying to save my life. In our faith journeys, everyone loves to hear about the blessings of faith and the adventure of a new life in Christ, but faith isn't hard during the good times. Faith is hard when we need it most. "I trust God" is easy to say and easy to believe when the mortgage is paid and everyone is healthy. "It's time to trust God" is harder to hear and almost impossible to believe when the money is gone and the doctor says the word *inoperable*. Biblical instructions are like diving instructions. They aren't always fun, and they don't always center on the adventure. Instead, they are taught for those moments when you most need faith.

> For by these He has granted to us His precious and magnificent promises, so that by them you may become partakers of the divine nature, having escaped the corruption that is in the world by lust. Now for this very reason also, applying all diligence,

in your faith supply moral excellence, and in your moral excellence, knowledge, and in your knowledge, self-control, and in your self-control, perseverance, and in your perseverance, godliness, and in your godliness, brotherly kindness, and in your brotherly kindness, love. For if these qualities are yours and are increasing, they render you neither useless nor unfruitful in the true knowledge of our Lord Jesus Christ.

—2 Peter 1:4–8 (NASU)

In this passage, Peter is telling the church to pursue spiritual transformation and become *partakers of the divine nature.* He's talking about character needed for the maturing faith that's willing to move toward the image of Christ. How? Peter says it's by *applying all diligence.* We will not stumble into the image of Christ or accidently fall into it. We must *apply all diligence* as God transforms our nature and frees us through His divine grace. He calls every believer to accept the goal of being conformed to the image of Christ for the glory of God.

Lives we control are incapable of experiencing the power of God's will.

Peter's own life reflected many of the pitfalls and lessons we will experience in our spiritual journeys. Peter had highs and lows, but his journey ultimately prepared him for the life God had called him to live. God has designed each of us with exactly what we need to live a deep and extraordinary faith. Yet so many of us are disappointed with the relationship we have with God, or we are willing to be content in the belief that this is all there is to a life in Christ. How did we get to that point? Somewhere along the way, we decided to remain in control of our lives. What we discover is that *lives we control are incapable of experiencing the power of God's will.*

What does a life we control look like?

In the book of Matthew, we see dialogue between Jesus and His disciples where He begins to speak about the importance of His death. Peter quickly rebukes Jesus for talking about His death. It is evident here that, while Peter was associated with Jesus, they did not want the same things. Peter and many of the disciples think they have bought into a sure thing. They believe that Jesus is the Messiah, a military leader capable of defeating the Roman authorities ruling their lands. Peter believes that God's plans will be best achieved through Jesus physically ruling from an earthly throne. You see, Jesus' death is not in Peter's plans. Peter tells Jesus what He ought to do and how He ought to do it. Peter is thinking about how God's will would interfere with his personal plans.

> But He turned and told Peter, "Get behind Me, Satan! You are an offense to Me because you're not thinking about God's concerns, but man's."
> —Matthew 16:23 (HCSB)

Peter wasn't willing to give God control of his plans. He was sure he knew what was best for his life and for Jesus' ministry. He was ultimately demonstrating a trust issue with God's plans. He could not *apply with all diligence* the faithfulness to follow the plans of God because he was struggling with his trust in Jesus' decisions.

Peter did not accept the fact that *God's vantage point gives Him a unique advantage to lead our lives.* Every life on the planet at some point, at some level, wrestles with these questions: Do I trust God? Do I believe God's vantage point gives Him a unique advantage to lead my life? Do I trust God when I disagree with what He says? Do I trust God when He seemingly makes no sense? Do I trust God when He asks me to take the first step? Do I trust God when no one else agrees with Him?

Now, we might sincerely want to trust God. In theory, trusting God is the easy response, but do we trust God with our most intimate relationships, those turning points in our careers, or with the problems that keep us up at night? Can I trust God when I don't get what I desire or what I, and others, deem to be the only socially acceptable option? Can we trust God when we don't understand why He moved in one direction when we feel He ought to be moving in a different direction? We think it's our situation, and we're convinced that our option is the only loving, compassionate, reasonable one available. Time and time again, when this happens, it pushes us to believe that if God is a trustworthy God, He will come through with the results we want. I'm afraid we live in a generation where our trust is results-driven. But trust in God is larger than physical results! Far too often, we celebrate when we get what we want and start to doubt God altogether when we don't see the answers to our prayers. Physical results are way too small a gauge when it comes to God's will in our lives. We simply can't know what He knows.

God's vantage point gives Him a unique advantage to lead our lives.

Trust is a full-time characteristic from our side of the relationship and a full-time expectation from God's side of the relationship. I would never tell my wife, "You can expect a trusting relationship on Mondays, Wednesdays, Thursdays, and Sundays, but trust is off the table the other three days of the week." Trust is best seen through consistency. But what happens when God is not asking us to trust Him in situations that are out of our hands, such as natural disasters or health, but in times when we face a decision where we have a choice?

"God, you want me to go to seminary, but I've got a family to support. I mean, I can't just leave my job and go back to school. I suppose I could, but there's a lot to a decision like this. It's way more than just a step of faith. I mean, how can I ask my family to support me through school again? We just bought this house. I don't want the kids to go without the things they want. If they were younger, I would do it, but today, I can't just throw everything away."

"Give up this relationship? I don't think so. This is the best relationship I've ever been in. We met at church, and everyone's always telling me to date a Christian. Yes, there are some problems, and living together doesn't seem to be helping, but I just don't care. We love each other, and that's all that matters to me!"

"Ten percent! I know that's what the Bible says, but when they made that rule, gas wasn't $3.50 a gallon. I'd be giving up 40 percent of my income. I mean, between tithing and income taxes, I'd have to change my standard of living. Plus that money is already spent. My family has expectations!"

"Mission field! My child, a missionary? I should be proud, *but what if something happens?* God put our family in America. He gave me children here in the States. Why would He want to take my child to another part of the world? I can't take the chance of them being eaten by a lion, stabbed by some half-naked native, or left suffering by some third-world disease no one's ever heard of. No, that's too much to ask!"

"This deal would bring in six months of my salary. All right, it's not ethical, but no one's convinced me it's illegal. And in this industry— an industry, God, that *You* opened the doors for me to get into—this is just standard practice. Besides, it's what the boss wants me to do. I'm following his directions. The moral repercussions are on him. I'm only doing it so I can take the family on a cruise. With the amount of time I had to spend on this deal, it's the least I can do."

At some point, God is going to ask us to do things we don't understand. He will ask us to face situations where our trust isn't seen in the midst of tragedy or crisis but in our obedience to step out in faith and do something. Some situations where we're called to trust God are out of our control, like the death of a loved one or the company's layoffs, but what do we do with the moments where we must make a decision?

Our ability to diligently pursue the image of Christ begins when we decide to trust God, leaving us with the question: what does trust in God look like? When we trust God, we are weighing the value of what's being surrendered from our lives against the value of God's trustworthiness. We're comparing God's promises with potential earthly gains. Ultimately, Scripture shows us that God's promises are so much more, revealing that we can't accurately compare the value of what we're surrendering to what He promises. Like Peter, what we're really deciding is this: do I believe God is trustworthy?

Even before he faced the message of Jesus' death, Peter had to deal with Jesus' invitation to trust Him. In front of a crowd with his reputation on the line, with his career on the line, Peter had to decide if he trusted Jesus.

> As the crowd was pressing in on Jesus to hear God's word, He was standing by Lake Gennesaret. (ghen-nay-sar-et': the Sea of Galilee) He saw two boats at the edge of the lake; the fishermen had left them and were washing their nets. He got into one of the boats, which belonged to Simon, and asked him to put out a little from the land. Then He sat down and was teaching the crowds from the boat. When He had finished speaking, He said to Simon, "Put out into deep water and let down your nets for a catch."
> —Luke 5:1–4 (HCSB)

Jesus had a much bigger purpose than catching fish, but Simon Peter didn't know that. What he knew was that he and his crew had been out all night, hadn't caught a thing, and had already washed and stored the nets for the day. He was thinking,

"You're a great preacher, but you don't know anything about fishing. And with all these potential clients staring at us, you want me to do something that everyone knows is foolish. No one fishes during the day; the fish have swum to the bottom. Jesus, You may know a whole lot more about other things, but I know more about this specific situation. My reputation as a fisherman is on the line. My abilities and my competence are going to be questioned if I listen to You."

But have you ever said, "God, you know how to create a world, but you don't know too much about finances in this economy! You don't know about starting a second career at my age. You don't understand how hard it is to find a relationship in this town, to find anyone who'll love me!"

In this moment, Peter had to decide if Jesus was trustworthy. It's the same decision we must make. Do you trust Jesus enough to follow Him? Salvation is free, but following Jesus will eventually cost us something!

Peter had to decide if he trusted Him enough to pay the price of following Him

> "Master," Simon replied, "we've worked hard all night long and caught nothing! But at Your word, I'll let down the nets." When they did this, they caught a great number of fish, and their nets began to tear. So they signaled to their partners in the other boat to come and help them; they came and filled both boats so full that they began to sink.
> —Luke 5:5–7 (HCSB)

What Peter found out was that when we trust God, His faithfulness exceeds our expectations! What happened in the boat wasn't what Peter thought would happen. In fact, it was more than Peter had hoped would happen. Ultimately—and this is where it starts to hit real close to home—what Jesus did for Peter was done differently from how Peter would have done it and differently from how he believed it should happen. Many times, Jesus will take a different path than the one we're expecting Him to take. Then we question His directions because we have focused on what we think ought to happen and have stopped looking to see what God wants.

As a follower of Christ, here's the best part about this passage: Peter's trust took the attention away from Peter and put it on Jesus. The crowd saw God's power in Peter's decision. How did it affect Peter?

> When Simon Peter saw this, he fell at Jesus' knees and
> said, "Go away from me, because I'm a sinful man,
> Lord!" For he and all those with him were amazed at
> the catch of fish they took, and so were James and
> John, Zebedee's sons, who were Simon's partners.
> "Don't be afraid," Jesus told Simon. "From now on
> you will be catching people!"
> —Luke 5:8–10 (HCSB)

Peter exclaims, "Jesus, You're awesome! I can't be in Your presence! You're amazing, and I'm such a sinner! Jesus, You are Lord. Please go. We are not worthy to have You with us!"

Just like Isaiah hundreds of years before him, Peter saw the power and authority of Jesus, and it caused him to reflect on the sin in his life.

> Then I said: Woe is me, for I am ruined, because I
> am a man of unclean lips and live among a people
> of unclean lips, and because my eyes have seen the
> King, the Lord of Hosts.
> —Isaiah 6:5 (HCSB)

Another possible reason for Peter's response is based on the idea that he was about to say no to Jesus' request and follow his own wisdom about fishing. Reluctantly, Peter weighed the cost and decided to do it. Maybe he was embarrassed by how close he came to refusing. "No, Jesus, I let You borrow my boat. I've done enough." But he weighed his options. It wouldn't cost him much to comply. He may have faced a little embarrassment had God not come through, but over time, he'd get over it and forget any cost that came from trusting. Ultimately, Peter did it, but reflecting on his reluctance might have driven him to his confession.

I'm afraid most of our decisions to trust God are weighted by the cost of what's being surrendered, not by the value of God's trustworthiness. When we're young and poor, we say, "Wherever You lead, I'll go!" Now we're older, and the stakes are higher. The cost is much greater, and the consequences are much deeper and longer lasting. Now our trust in God's will is causing us great tension!

"'Don't be afraid,' Jesus told Simon. 'From now on you will be catching people!'" (Luke 5:10 HCSB).

Up to this point, the cost of following Jesus had been manageable, but now Jesus was asking for a career change. The cost of following would be tremendous, and the value of what Jesus was asking him to surrender was huge. It was so high that it stopped being about the cost of what Peter was surrendering and became about the value of the One asking!

When it comes to trusting God, the value of what God is asking us to give Him doesn't matter. It only matters that we believe God is trustworthy. Because if we trust Him and believe that He is trustworthy, the value of the thing surrendered is nothing compared to the value of what He offers in return!

"God, you don't understand. This is valuable. The price is too high. You are asking too much!" But God is telling us, "The issue is not the value of what's in your hand." He simply asks us, "Am I trustworthy?"

If God says, "Give Me ten dollars, and I'll open up the floodgates of heaven," we'd respond, "Okay! If God comes through and blesses me, that's great, but if He doesn't, then it's only ten dollars. So okay, God, here's ten dollars."

God then ask us, "Do you believe I'm trustworthy?"

We may think about it for a minute but then respond, "Yes, I believe You're trustworthy and will honor this gift of ten dollars."

"Ok, now," God says, "Give Me 10 percent, and I'll open up the floodgates of heaven."

With the request change, so does our tone. "I can't. What You're asking from me is too much!"

The illustration is not a money issue, it's a trust issue. It doesn't matter about the example because in the end, the value of the item changed. God didn't change. If He's trustworthy with ten dollars, is He trustworthy with 10 percent? If God is trustworthy with an hour of service to Him a month, is He trustworthy with an hour a week?

> "Don't be afraid," Jesus told Simon. "From now on you will be catching people!" Then they brought the boats to land, left everything, and followed Him.
> —Luke 5:10–11 (HCSB)

The cost was huge! They left their boats and walked away from the only career they had ever known and into a life of ministry they didn't understand. But in their eyes, Jesus was trustworthy.

What is it that you know God wants you to do, but you've been reluctant to trust Him? Do you believe Jesus is trustworthy? Is he trustworthy enough to *apply all diligence* to your faith?

Peter finally got to this point. He still wasn't perfect. Over time, for instance, we'd see that he wasn't sure how he felt about Gentiles. But as Peter grew in his faith, he did arrive at the point where he boldly stood before His community and let everyone know Jesus Christ was his Lord. That confession took him to a cross.

> "I assure you: When you were young, you would tie your belt and walk wherever you wanted. But when you grow old, you will stretch out your hands and someone else will tie you and carry you where you don't want to go." He said this to signify by what kind of death he would glorify God. After saying this, He told him, "Follow Me!"
> —John 21:18–19 (HCSB)

And on the day Peter lost his life, he didn't deny the Lord. He stood up and proclaimed the greatness of his God! We are not always going to know where God's will is taking us. Our trust in Christ says, "I don't have to fully understand what He wants." As we mature spiritually and journey deeper in our faith, we will come to the point where we say, "I don't need to know what God wants before I say yes. I say yes because He is my God!

In our focal passage, Peter was telling those early believers—and he is telling us today—that the passionate pursuit of conforming to the image of Christ involves *diligence*. No quitters! Have you ever watched someone at work or in sports give up and quit? For whatever reason, they lose heart and come to a conscience decision to simply stop working toward their goals. It's almost sickening for us to watch someone quit. We get uncomfortable and pity them. We want to motivate them and encourage them to press on toward their goal. As Christians, we need to be burdened by spiritual apathy.

We're not left to wonder about how this pursuit takes place in our lives, however. In our focal passage, Peter gives us seven specific and definable characteristics that build on each other and lead us to the very image of Christ:

- moral excellence

- knowledge

- self-control

- perseverance

- godliness

- brotherly kindness

- love

We are not to sit and expect these things to magically happen. Peter said we must *supply*, which takes a conscience effort and intentional action to feed our faith.

In this book, we will carefully examine each of those seven characteristics. It's an exciting journey from salvation, or wherever you are in your own spiritual path, to being radically and eternally transformed into the image of Christ. Do we ever complete that journey? Are we ever perfectly transformed? Well, that's the challenge that awaits us!

Study Questions

Intro video for group study can be found at
www.myjourneydeeper.com

1. How would you define *applying all diligence* in your relationship with the Lord?

2. What does a life we control look like in contrast to a life God controls?

3. Why does God's vantage point give Him a unique advantage to lead our lives?

4. How do you process that salvation is free but following Jesus will eventually cost you something?

5. What did you learn from this chapter, and how can you apply it to your life?

6. What areas do you need to pray about or improve in your walk with Jesus?

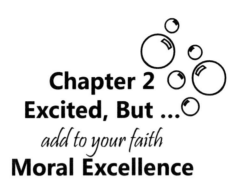

Chapter 2
Excited, But ...

add to your faith
Moral Excellence

After months of classes and hours upon hours of training in confined water dives, I was finally certified for my first open-water dive in the gulf. We arrived early in the morning at the dive shop and loaded our equipment onto the boat. It was a charter dive split between new divers from our college class and experienced divers from around the area. We were diving to a popular wreck resting between thirty to fifty feet deep. I'd love to tell you the weather was perfect, but late April in northwest Florida made the water cold. I was using old tanks and a rented regulator, but most importantly, I was wearing a new wet suit! It was cold, and I hate to be cold.

Approximately an hour after we left the docks, we arrived at the dive site, and everyone began to suit up. I put my wet suit on first, then I checked my buoyancy compensator vest, regulators, and tanks. I began to gear up to back-roll off the side of the boat and into my first adventure. As my turn approached, I strapped on my fins, followed by my mask, and tested my regulator one more time. When the deckhand pointed to me, I took my position on the side of the boat, said a silent prayer that I wouldn't hit my head on the tank, and flipped off the boat and into the water.

My day had finally arrived. I was a diver! I swam over to the line we were following down to the wreck and started fin-kicking as hard as I could, but I kept popping back to the top. The deckhand yelled out, "What's wrong?" I didn't want to yell back, "I don't know!" ...but I didn't know. I thought through everything and went through a mental checklist from everything we had covered in the classes, trying to recall all the information I had received to become a diver, but I couldn't figure it out. The deckhand asked if I had enough weight on my belt, and I realized—no belt! In my excitement to start diving, I forgot an essential piece of equipment: my weight belt! Embarrassed but not discouraged, I swam back to the boat, got the belt, and embarked on my adventure.

Many believers inside the church find themselves in a similar situation in their faith. We can be so excited about being a believer that we miss a few necessary pieces to making the journey successful. In churches across America, attendance has long been the standard for Christian maturity. It didn't so much matter what someone did away from the church. As long as you "go, give, and get seen," you were good in the eyes of the church. I absolutely believe that church attendance is important to every person's spiritual journey. Scripture clearly and repeatedly encourages us not to forsake meeting together. Yet if we are ever going to fully understand what it means to move beyond salvation to reflecting the image of Christ, we cannot stop the journey at attending church; we must fully understand what it means to *be the church*.

Step 1: Moral excellence is the God-given ability to perform heroic deeds.

In our focal passage, 2 Peter 1:4–8, Peter begins the journey from salvation to reflecting the image of Christ through a natural and important starting point: moral excellence. After all, many unbelievers define Christianity by a handful of virtuous acts. Even those who grew up attending church got the message that maturity in Christ is defined by a person's stance on alcohol, smoking, and public moral decency. So it seems a natural first step when Peter urges believers toward moral excellence.

Before we self-righteously check off this first characteristic and move on, however, we need to determine exactly what constitutes moral excellence. Peter is *not* talking about a moral attitude or virtuous desires. It's not as simple as saying, "No problem. I like moral things and dislike evil things." Instead, moral excellence is the harnessed power to live a lifestyle of excellence. In fact, the classic Greek definition of this word is much different from a mere legalistic view of good and bad. *Arete* (ar-et'-ay), which we interpret as "moral excellence" (or "virtue"), is the God-given ability to perform heroic deeds. That puts a different slant on this concept, doesn't it?

Moral excellence is the God-given ability to perform heroic deeds.

Today, heroes come in many different forms. We create heroes from athletes, actors, and artists who are able to do things we can only imagine in our minds. Thankfully, true heroes still exist in our generation through the men and women who protect our shores and rush into burning buildings for people they don't know. Heroes are built through exceptional skill or unwavering character, but Scripture describes moral heroes as those believers willing to live a life committed to the moral excellence of God.

Moral excellence turns godly parents into heroes for their children. It turns average Christ followers into heroes for their neighbors and friends. It turns students totally committed to Christ into heroes on their campuses and in their homes. It turns singles into heroes as they morally stand in a compromising society. Moral excellence turns Christians into heroes for a culture that is searching to see lives transformed by the truth of moral absolutes.

Daniel is a great biblical example of a man who exemplified moral excellence. His life was a series of ups and downs but is forever defined by the heroic moral stand he made for God. His life was incredible, especially when contrasted against his culture.

The Babylonian Empire had captured Israel, and Daniel, along with many others, was transported to Babylon for indoctrination into the local culture. While in Babylon, Daniel began to distinguish himself from others with an attitude of excellence in such a way that he became a provincial administrator. By the time the Medo-Persians defeated the Babylonian Empire, Daniel had become so distinguished that he was made governor, serving in a role equivalent to a prime minister. You can probably imagine that Daniel's rise to power over the local leaders made him a political and personal target.

> Then this Daniel began distinguishing himself among the commissioners and satraps because he possessed an extraordinary spirit, and the king planned to appoint him over the entire kingdom. Then the commissioners and satraps began trying to find a ground of accusation against Daniel in regard to government affairs; but they could find no ground of accusation or evidence of corruption, inasmuch as he was faithful, and no negligence or corruption was to be found in him.
> —Daniel 6:3–4 (NASU)

The anger of these men toward Daniel pushed them to look for anything they could find against Daniel. Yet with all their resources, they could not find any corruption in his life. Daniel was living a life of moral excellence; however, they did notice a common thread running throughout Daniel's life. It was one thing that seemed to be so constant, something so tangible that it defined his everyday life. Daniel was passionate about leading a life that pursued the glory of his God.

So these local leaders designed a trap. They went to the king and talked him into writing a law that recognized the king as a god for thirty days. The decree stated that no one could pray to any other god except the king for thirty days, or they would face the consequences of being thrown into the lion's den. The king enacted the law, stating that now even he, the king, could not reverse it. Meanwhile, our little band of local leaders staked out Daniel's life.

> Now when Daniel knew that the document was signed, he entered his house (now in his roof chamber he had windows open toward Jerusalem); and he continued kneeling on his knees three times a day, praying and giving thanks before his God, **as he had been doing previously**.
> —Daniel 6:10 (NASU; emphasis by author)

When Daniel heard about the new law, he went home and did what he was accustomed to doing every day. He went to his roof chamber that had windows open toward Jerusalem (where he could be seen, of course) and prayed as usual, giving thanks to God.

With the law in place and his career and life most likely on the line, Daniel knew he was now at the point of a critical decision. He was forced to decide if he was going to live the life of a moral hero or justify his way out. Justification sounds good, and it's the compromise many people might make. Daniel might have thought, *On the one hand, I can't pray to the king because I would be disobeying God by worshiping another god; but on the other hand, if I worship and pray to God, I would lose my position in the government and not be able to share my testimony or influence government. So I'm just not going to pray to anyone. For the next thirty days, I'm simply going to remain spiritually neutral.* Sounds good, right? Spiritual justification may ease our conscience for a time, but it breaks the heart of God.

Let me show you the life of a hero. Daniel did pray to God just as he had always done, and he did get thrown into the lions' den, leading us to assume that he would die a very courageous death. Remember, Daniel didn't know that God was going to rescue him from the lions. He thought that night would be his last night on earth; however, God had a different plan for Daniel, and what happened next was simply miraculous.

Scripture tells us that all night long, Daniel slept soundly with the lions while the king paced back and forth dealing with his own conscience. The next morning, the king ran to see what had happened to Daniel. The king wanted to see if Daniel's God had been able to do what he could not. He expected to see the death of a courageous man but hoped to see the protective power of Daniel's God.

> Then Daniel spoke to the king, "O king, live forever! My God sent His angel and shut the lions' mouths and they have not harmed me, inasmuch as I was found innocent before Him; and also toward you, O king, I have committed no crime." Then the king was very pleased and gave orders for Daniel to be taken up out of the den. So Daniel was taken up out of the den and no injury whatever was found on him, because he had trusted in his God. The king then gave orders, and they brought those men who had maliciously accused Daniel, and they cast them, their children and their wives into the lions' den; and they had not reached the bottom of the den before the lions overpowered them and crushed all their bones.
> —Daniel 6:21–24 (NASU)

Daniel testified to the king about the power of God in protecting him from the lions. He ordered for Daniel to be taken out of the lions' den and had the men who had accused Daniel thrown into the den. When the king saw the power of God at work, he realized that the voices he once trusted were empty. He began to see the lack of character and faith of the men he once trusted with his life.

We can identify with struggling to know who to believe. It's difficult to do the right thing. We have so many voices telling us to compromise, fit in, and go with the flow and so few voices challenging us to stand with moral excellence or to take personal responsibility for our mistakes. Many people acknowledge their wrongdoing only if they get caught.

Shortly after the king witnessed the protection of a loving God, these once-trusted voices—these local leaders, these old boys who thought they had beat the system—experienced the discipline of a protecting God! As Scripture tells us, the king threw every one of his advisors, along with their entire families, into the lions' den. God protects those who walk in obedience. Someone might ask, "Why doesn't the church of today see that kind of power from God?" One explanation might be that today, God doesn't see that kind of moral excellence from His church.

Of course, the story doesn't end with the death of Daniel's enemies. The great lasting legacy of the story is not Daniel's rescue but the king's second decree.

> Then Darius the king wrote to all the peoples, nations and men of every language who were living in all the land: "May your peace abound! I make a decree that in all the dominion of my kingdom men are to fear and tremble before the God of Daniel; For He is the living God and enduring forever, and His kingdom is one which will not be destroyed, and His dominion will be forever. He delivers and rescues and performs signs and wonders in heaven and on earth, Who has also delivered Daniel from the power of the lions."
> —Daniel 6:25–27 (NASU)

One man living with moral excellence humbled a king to acknowledge God, exposing every man, woman, and child to the knowledge of Yahweh, the one true God. Moral excellence may not expand your fame, but it will move you toward your spiritual goal of conforming to the image of Christ for the purpose of bringing glory to God. God used extreme circumstances in Daniel's story to teach humility to the king, but sometimes he uses different methods.

I don't remember where I first heard this story, but I've always remembered the point. A young seminarian was excited about preaching his first sermon in his home church. After three years in seminary, he felt adequately prepared. When he was introduced to the congregation, he walked boldly to the pulpit, his head high, radiating self-confidence, but he stumbled reading the Scriptures and then lost his train of thought halfway through the message. He began to panic, so he did the safest thing. He quickly ended the message, prayed, and walked dejectedly from the pulpit, his head down, his self-assurance gone. Later, one of the godly elders whispered to the embarrassed young man, "If you had gone up to the pulpit the way you came down, you might have come down the way you went up." The elder was right. God still resists the proud but gives grace to the humble.

In *Each New Day*, Corrie Ten Boom tells the story about meeting Sadhu Sundar Singh, an Indian Christian missionary, in Europe after he had completed a tour around the world. Someone asked him, "Doesn't it do harm, you getting so much honor?" Then Sadhu answered, "No. The donkey went into Jerusalem, and they put garments on the ground before him. He was not proud. He knew it was not done to honor him, but for Jesus, who was sitting on his back. When people honor me, I know it is not me, but the Lord, who does the job."

It amazes me how often we as Christ followers have forgotten that truth. Daniel had all the power but had humbled himself enough to be used by God. Today, we have an unwritten mind-set leading us to believe that God is lucky to have us on His side. God's not lucky to have us. He made us! The most gifted person in the bride of Christ (the church) is still a simple tool in the hand of the Master.

I'm afraid the church has followed the world in creating heroes based on our preferences and not based on God's standards. Inside the subculture of Christianity, we've turned a handful of successful pastors into rock stars and expect Christian artists to live with the same social flare as secular artists. I believe one day, when Christ comes again, the biggest heroes in heaven will be people we've never heard of! Moral excellence is not defined by an arbitrary standard we create for ourselves but is established by God's Word and lived out only by those in pursuit of His image. Many years ago, Isaiah told us what qualities cause God to "look favorably" on us.

> My hand made all these things, and so they all came into being. This is the Lord's declaration. I will look favorably on this kind of person: one who is humble, submissive in spirit, and who trembles at My word.
> —Isaiah 66:2 (HCSB)

Daniel is one amazing picture of moral excellence, but thankfully, he is not alone. Over the years, God has used a small passage in Luke to remind me that moral excellence never starts on the outside. God-driven moral excellence always begins on the inside but will eventually prove itself to be empty and spiritually hollow if it does not begin from a submissive and surrendered heart.

> He also told this parable to some who trusted in themselves that they were righteous and looked down on everyone else: "Two men went up to the temple complex to pray, one a Pharisee and the other a tax collector. The Pharisee took his stand and was praying like this: 'God, I thank You that I'm not like other people —greedy, unrighteous, adulterers, or even like this tax collector. I fast twice a week; I give a tenth of everything I get.' But the tax collector, standing far off, would not even raise his eyes to heaven but kept striking his chest and saying, 'God, turn Your wrath from me —a sinner!' I tell you, this one went down to his house justified rather than the other; because everyone who exalts himself will be humbled, but the one who humbles himself will be exalted."
> —Luke 18:9–14 (HCSB)

One of the most penetrating lines in this entire passage is the opening statement. "He also told this parable to some who trusted in themselves that they were righteous and looked down on everyone else." Jesus was looking at a crowd of people who were impressed with their own righteousness. He saw their actions, but He was really looking at their hearts. We have fooled ourselves into believing a lie. We can say to ourselves, "I'm way too nice, way too educated, way too religiously connected, and way too middle-class wealthy to ever face the wrath of God." We believe we know all the right answers and that God is happy that we've just taken the time to acknowledge His existence. This kind of arrogance is a problem that has plagued God's people throughout history. We're reminded of the Lord's lesson for Samuel (and for us, of course). "Man does not see what the LORD sees, for man sees what is visible, but the LORD sees the heart" (1 Samuel 16:7 HCSB).

God sees everything and knows everything, but He's most concerned about the condition of our hearts. He knew that many of the religious people around Him were extremely proud of their public lives. The crowd around Jesus included religious leaders, men scattered around the crowd allowing everyone the privilege of watching them. They were proud of themselves! But Jesus knew the people there, like the billions who have since read these words, were all looking around, trying to decide where they rated on the holiness scale. "Where do I fit in? Who do I look like?"

Jesus made sure every person could find themselves somewhere in His words. He described the Pharisee perching himself on the temple steps as he began to wax poetically about his own righteous deeds. The Pharisee's statement burned in the hearts of some people in the crowd. They had often made similar statements in their own prayers.

Can I give you a spiritual nugget? There is nothing more useless than spiritually showing off for someone else. I don't care if you think you're ten steps ahead of others spiritually. It's like comparing the beauty of two monkfish (the ugliest fish on the planet). The only spiritual standard that matters is the unattainable standard of perfection. According to that standard, all of us stand condemned except for the free gift of God's grace. Righteous acts, such as the spiritual disciplines we find in Scripture, are not to be used as a measure of our own righteousness but as opportunities to draw closer to God. Daniel didn't pray for others to see; he prayed to draw himself closer to God. The Pharisee was trying to impress God, like contestants on a dating game show shouting, "Pick me!" One dangerous trap for many lifelong believers is that we can start to believe that God brought us from death to life but that we'll take it from there. We freely give God our eternity, but we refuse to give Him our life. We can't do much about eternity or life after death. We like the sound of heaven over hell, so we buy into a heavenly eternity. The problem begins when we overlook that salvation is surrendering our lives in exchange for eternity in His presence. We do not get the option to give God our eternity without giving Him our lives.

Jesus then contrasted the heart of the Pharisee with the brokenness of a tax collector, a man who recognized his sins and owned them. Truthfully, his sins were much more public than what we know about the sins of Daniel. Heroically, he did not justify his actions but confessed them before God. The tax collector had a completely different posture of worship and need. He didn't see himself as a jewel in God's crown. In fact, his time of worship was bringing him to a point of pure confession. He didn't justify his actions or hope God would forget about them. Instead, he confessed his sin before God and asked for mercy.

The closer we get to God, the less able we are to see our own glory in light of His. The tax collector was in the presence of God; therefore, he knew he couldn't impress God. He simply needed to humble himself before a Holy God.

If you haven't spent much time in David's confession in Psalm 51, take a few moments and reread one of the most honest and broken confessions ever recorded.

> Be gracious to me, God, according to Your faithful love; according to Your abundant compassion, blot out my rebellion. Wash away my guilt, and cleanse me from my sin. For I am conscious of my rebellion, and my sin is always before me. Against You —You

alone —I have sinned and done this evil in Your sight. So You are right when You pass sentence; You are blameless when You judge. Indeed, I was guilty when I was born; I was sinful when my mother conceived me.

Surely You desire integrity in the inner self, and You teach me wisdom deep within. Purify me with hyssop, and I will be clean; wash me, and I will be whiter than snow. Let me hear joy and gladness; let the bones You have crushed rejoice. Turn Your face away from my sins and blot out all my guilt. God, create a clean heart for me and renew a steadfast spirit within me. Do not banish me from Your presence or take Your Holy Spirit from me. Restore the joy of Your salvation to me, and give me a willing spirit. Then I will teach the rebellious Your ways, and sinners will return to You.
—Psalm 51:1–13 (HCSB)

You may identify with Daniel, the tax collector, or maybe the Pharisee, but no matter where you find yourself as you read through this book, I want you to remember one inescapable truth: *confession is not a sign of spiritual weakness but of spiritual strength.*

When it comes to moral excellence, the truth is that many of us have failed at some point, and the most heroic thing we can do is confess and repent! Falling is not failure. Spiritual failure is when we refuse to confess and admit that we are not perfect. The spiritually weak refuse to admit they need accountability because they believe their reputation and pride are more important than doing whatever it takes to be conformed to the image of Christ.

Confession is not a sign of spiritual weakness but of spiritual strength.

After completing my embarrassing first dive, I knew we were in our surface interval and had a few hours before our next dive. Along with being certified in basic scuba diving, I was also getting a certification in night diving. Diving at night is amazing because of the focus it brings. You can only see what your light shows you. All distractions are gone. It's truly a moment of single focus. In our lives, we can become so cluttered with life that we do not focus on what's essential. I want to encourage you to spend some time asking God to shine His light on one thing in your life He wants to transform.

That night, with the memories of the morning dives fresh in my mind, I was still holding my weight belt as I once again waited my turn to flip over the side. When I heard my name called, I took my position and showed the deckhand my belt. He grinned and said, "No, sir, I wasn't going to ask you if you remembered your weights. I wanted to make sure you remembered your light." Smiling, I held up the light and flipped over the side.

Study Questions

Intro video for group study can be found at
www.myjourneydeeper.com

1. Discuss the author's definition for the characteristic of moral excellence: moral excellence is the God-given ability to perform heroic deeds.

2. Does the church have a proper view of moral excellence?

3. What impresses you about Daniel's life?

4. Why is spiritual justification such a dangerous issue for people of faith?

5. Why do we see confession as a spiritual weakness instead of a spiritual strength?

6. What did you learn from this chapter, and how can you apply it to your life?

7. What areas do you need to pray about or improve in your walk with Jesus?

Chapter 3
What Do I Do Now?

**Step 1: Moral excellence is the God-given
ability to perform heroic deeds.**

add to your faith
Knowledge

One day, Todd, Andy, their dad, and I were headed out to dive at some sights off the shore of Pensacola Beach. We were going a few miles out, and the seas were pretty rough that day. Dr. Mignerey told us that visibility might be limited because of the silt in the water being stirred up by the currents. "Boys, hold onto the anchor line all the way down, and once you're on the bottom, visibility ought to clear up for you to enjoy the dive. If not, come up, and we'll find a new site."

Once in the water, I was the last to head down. I swam over to the anchor line and began to fin-kick down. The current was really strong and much like the pull you feel from undertow. I was really getting knocked around. Somewhere in the middle of the descent, however, I let go of the rope to clear the pressure out of my ears, and the current got me. I was suddenly and unexpectedly pulled away from the line and quickly became disoriented. Unable to see, I realized that I didn't know which way was up or down. The current had twisted me, and the pressure from the water left me unable to figure out which way to swim. I didn't know what to do. I inflated my BC (buoyancy compensator vest) and curled up in a ball to feel which way I would begin to float. After just a few seconds, I was able to determine which way was up and began swimming for the surface.

Those few minutes when I didn't know where I was or which way to go were the most frightening parts of that dive. Once I had my direction, even though I couldn't see where I was going, I knew it was right, and that knowledge gave me peace. In our faith journey, when we don't know where to go or what to do, we need knowledge. Peter tells us that once we have added moral excellence to our faith, we need to add knowledge. What is knowledge?

Step 2: Knowledge is the truth of God properly comprehended and applied.

My family loves to travel. Through mission trips and family vacations, we've had the opportunity to see a lot of the world. Experiencing different cultures, seeing amazing sights, and marking off great adventures are all nice, but we judge every vacation by one standard alone: the food! When we reminisce about trips and experiences, we usually begin with something like, "Wasn't that the trip when we ate that amazing seafood?" or "You remember that's the trip where Mom got the raw steak, and the waiter was so embarrassed." Our family is so serious about the meals we eat while we're traveling that we've planned entire vacations around favorite restaurants. Personally, I'm not sure if my wife likes going to Israel to walk where Jesus walked or for the hummus. (Just kidding, Lori!)

Knowledge is the truth of God properly comprehended and applied.

While we joke about our love of food, we also know that food nourishes our body, just as the Word of God nourishes our souls. One of the original Greek words from our text paints a beautiful image of nourishment. The word *epichoregeo* (ep-ee-khor-ayg-eh'-o), which is interpreted "applying" or in some translations "add," tells us to feed our faith to the point of nourishment. In other words, faith that is not moving toward the image of Christ is starving. We as Christ followers need to crave the image of Christ in our lives and feed our faith with each of these characteristics. Knowledge given to us through the truths of God's Word allows us to have an expanded understanding of God's heart.

David said it this way in Psalm 63:1 (HCSB): "O God, You are my God; I shall seek You earnestly; My soul thirsts for You, my flesh yearns for You, in a dry and weary land where there is no water." The souls of all people are longing for the satisfaction of God. Not everyone recognizes their individual need for God, and many people find different short-term distractions to satisfy the void left by the absence of God's presence. Those in a relationship with Christ have discovered that our faith is starving for the intimacy that spiritual transformation brings into our lives.

In the last chapter, we learned to feed our faith with the moral excellence of living out the God-given ability to perform heroic deeds. Now Peter tells us we are to feed our moral excellence and allow it to be nourished by our pursuit of knowledge. There are two extreme views on how to deal with knowledge. On one hand, there are believers who are fired up and passionate for anything spiritual and religious. I have watched these believers passionately follow an empty path of feel-good promises and easy returns. For instance, we've all heard the TV evangelists who promise that by "following" God, everything in life will be easy. These messages are emotionally captivating and exciting to believe, but they seem to reject a repeated truth in Scripture that teaches just the opposite. In fact, the book of Acts tells us that Stephen discovered faithfulness to Jesus brought physical death, not money.

On the other hand, I've known biblically sound people so spiritually cold that they have become useless in the Kingdom's work—people educated and committed to know about the Word of God but who are not nourished by it. Spend any time around the church, and you will eventually run into a modern New Testament Pharisee. Jesus spent His entire ministry dealing with the religious leaders who could quote much of the Scriptures but had lost sight of God's heart. These modern-day New Testament Pharisees still present themselves as the religious elite but are completely incapable of nourishing others because of the coldness of their spirit.

Both extremes lead to an unhealthy faith and can be summed up this way: *knowledge without passion is* apathy, *but passion without knowledge is* heresy. If God's truth is not calling us to apathy or heresy, then we are left to ask, "To what knowledge has God called us to add to our virtue and faith?" I would define biblical knowledge as the truth of God properly comprehended and applied.

This knowledge is more than collected facts; it is applied truth. I can describe it to you. My mom was a great cook and wanted my brother and me to learn to eat all kinds of food; however, there was still one thing I just couldn't swallow. Even now...I can't eat eggs. Besides the smell and taste of eggs being completely revolting to me, I find the idea of eating a chicken's menstrual cycle just sickening. I liken it to Ezekiel's plea to God in Ezekiel 4, where he requests that he not have to eat food cooked over human excrement. Growing up, I always refused to eat eggs, and I would frequently get "the speech." "Don't you know that there are starving children around the world who would love to eat those eggs?" Now, I believed my mom. There has never been a time when I didn't believe that there were starving children around the world, and I felt sincerely sorry for them. But it wasn't until I crossed the borders of our country and saw children eating sewage to stay alive that I really understood starvation. Before that moment, I knew that it existed, but when I actually saw starving children, my understanding moved from facts to faces. My experience drove me to get involved with human rights issues around the world.

Just like I needed to let the knowledge of starvation take hold of my heart and lead me to act, Peter is telling us to apply this kind of comprehended truth to our faith. We need to move our knowledge of God from empty religious rhetoric to applied, accepted truth. What is so difficult about accepting God's knowledge? The foundational step in applying God's truth to our lives is accepting God's authority in our lives. We must surrender our will before we can accept His will. We are not decision makers in the kingdom of God. We are soldiers under the authority of our King, and He alone has the authority to give direction.

Jesus was the perfect example of a godly soldier in the kingdom's army. In the garden, He prayed to the Father for a different course of action, but He ended His prayer with the statement by which all decisions must be made: "not as I will, but as you will" (Matthew 26:39 NASU).

Moses also wanted to know God, and he entreated God with a prayer that needs to be the cry of our hearts if we desire to add God's truth to the moral excellence of our faith. "Now therefore, I pray You, if I have found favor in Your sight, let me know Your ways that I may know You, so that I may find favor in Your sight" (Exodus 33:13 NASU).

He accepted God's authority and had a passion to be intimate with God, so he asked God to reveal His ways. Moses showed us that if we want to know the heart of God, we must know the will of God. And if we want to be transformed into the image of God, we must live out the will of God.

So how do we know if we are following the will of God? Even grounded in the courage to live out a life in Christ, we all still find ourselves asking the question: what does God want with me? What is His will for my life? We are going to find the answer lived out in a young man who desired to obey God even though he didn't know much about God.

Josiah was king of Judah, the Southern Kingdom of Israel. His great grandfather Hezekiah was a godly king, but Hezekiah's son, Manasseh, was a wicked king. The moment Hezekiah died, Manasseh turned Judah away from God and into every kind of wicked practice and false religion you can think of. Any kind of religious idea was accepted, including child sacrifices. Manasseh reigned for fifty-five years until his son Amon became king. Amon ruled like his father, except he turned it up a notch. He only made it two years before a group in the palace rebelled and killed him, leaving his eight-year-old son, Josiah, to be the king.

Josiah's epitaph in 2 Kings 22:2 (NASU) reads, "He did right in the sight of the LORD and walked in all the way of his father David, nor did he turn aside to the right or to the left."

Josiah had a passion to know the God of Israel, the God of his great-grandfather, Hezekiah, and even greater grandfather, David. Josiah wanted to know God. The problem was that the temple had been destroyed and ransacked by his grandfather, Manasseh, so Josiah had never even seen a copy of the law and knew nothing about how to honor God. Amazingly, a "God thing" happened as Josiah was rebuilding the temple. Hilkiah, the high priest, found a copy of God's Word. Josiah told the handful of faithful priests to take the Word of God and tell Him what it said. The living and active Word of God affected Josiah, and once he heard from the heart of God, he realized just how far away Judah had gone from Him. It moved Josiah; it wounded him, and all he wanted to know was what God wanted him to do.

> When the king heard the words of the book of the law, he tore his clothes. Then the king commanded Hilkiah the priest, Ahikam the son of Shaphan, Achbor the son of Micaiah, Shaphan the scribe, and Asaiah the king's servant saying, "Go, inquire of the LORD for me and the people and all Judah concerning the words of this book that has been found, for great is the wrath of the LORD that burns against us, because our

fathers have not listened to the words of this book,
to do according to all that is written concerning us."
—2 Kings 22:11–13 (NASU)

Once Josiah heard God's Word, it brought him to a point of repentance and confession. Even though Josiah never personally engaged in these pagan practices, he was still broken by them. Why? Simply put, Josiah was more concerned with the glory of God than his own religious rights. And if you and I want to know the heart of God and be led by the will of God, we need to be more concerned about the reputation and glory of God than our religious freedoms and rights. I know we have freedoms in Christ. I know we have been granted rights in Christ. We have been granted incredible freedoms, privileges, and rights as a child of God, and we should never diminish these gifts. "Now the Lord is the Spirit; and where the Spirit of the Lord is, there is freedom" (2 Corinthians 3:17 HCSB).

Years ago at a college retreat, the organizer told the students, "We have one rule at the retreat: love God and do what you want." At first I was shocked by the broad liberty this goal seemed to give the group; however, when he reiterated the rule and stated, "Make sure you focus on the first part before you're drawn to start focusing on the second part of our rule," it all made sense. He was right. We don't need to focus on the rules and laws if we get the first part right: love God. Then what we want simply becomes a life that honors him.

Years later, I came to classify myself as a recovering Pharisee, one who had focused so much of my attention on the religious rules that I forgot to fall deeper in love with God. In response, I'm afraid I countered that movement with a swing too far the other direction, trying to prove that freedom in Christ meant I had freedom to do what I wanted to do. I finally understand God's heart on the war between freedom and obedience in an encounter between Jesus and the religious leaders trying to condemn Him:

> As He was teaching in one of the synagogues on the Sabbath, a woman was there who had been disabled by a spirit for over 18 years. She was bent over and

could not straighten up at all. When Jesus saw her, He called out to her, "Woman, you are free of your disability." Then He laid His hands on her, and instantly she was restored and began to glorify God. But the leader of the synagogue, indignant because Jesus had healed on the Sabbath, responded by telling the crowd, "There are six days when work should be done; therefore come on those days and be healed and not on the Sabbath day." But the Lord answered him and said, "Hypocrites! Doesn't each one of you untie his ox or donkey from the feeding trough on the Sabbath and lead it to water? Satan has bound this woman, a daughter of Abraham, for 18 years—shouldn't she be untied from this bondage on the Sabbath day?" When He had said these things, all His adversaries were humiliated, but the whole crowd was rejoicing over all the glorious things He was doing.
—Luke 13:10–17 (HCSB)

I want you to understand the pain of this woman. She lived every day hunched over while staring at the dirt as the curvature of her back was like the letter C. In constant pain, this little woman made her agonizing way to her local synagogue. Each step in her journey was burdened by the uneven stones in the road. Pain shot down her legs as her back continued to tighten up, unable to find relief even while doing the simplest tasks. Entering the synagogue for a time of worship, she had no idea what Jesus was about to do. She simply found her place in the crowd as one who has come to worship the God of Abraham, Isaac, and Jacob. In spite of the pain, she had come to worship! Nothing was going to keep her from being with her God and learning more about His heart. She didn't come to the synagogue to be seen or socialize with others. It was not for her enjoyment because every moment on her feet was excruciating! She didn't make that walk over and over again out of tradition or pressure. Week after week, she made this journey to worship with the God she loved.

But on this day, as Jesus began to speak to the crowd, He called to her! Can you imagine her embarrassment when Jesus called her out? She's unable to know that Jesus has looked into her heart and watched the last eighteen painful years of her life. His heart was breaking over the suffering she had endured, but what really grabbed His attention was her faith! Her worship was real; it was personal. She loved her God and hungered to hear His word.

Even with every eye in the synagogue looking at her, and even though she was feeling completely embarrassed, she and Jesus met. All she could do was stare right into His feet. Jesus said to her, "Woman, you are free of your disability." Can you imagine that moment? What an amazing moment! What a life-changing moment! What a moment of worship and praise! But all of that was stopped by the reaction of the synagogue leader. What was done to glorify God aggravated this leader. "There are six days when work should be done; therefore, come on those days, and be healed and not on the Sabbath day."

Now the Sabbath was instituted as a sign of God's covenant with His people. Just as God rested from His work of creation on the seventh day and set aside that day to reflect on the previous six, so each Jew was called to mirror that example by working six days and resting on the seventh. God's command to Moses was simple: "Remember to dedicate the Sabbath day: You are to labor six days and do all your work, but the seventh day is a Sabbath to the Lord your God" (Exodus 20:8–10 HCSB).

Over the years, however, a great mountain of various interpretations was laid upon this command, and its original purpose was obscured. The rabbis had established a system of thirty-nine categories of work, and each category was further divided into subcategories. The people couldn't distinguish between what God wanted and what the religious leaders thought. The synagogue official could only see the broken rule and completely dismissed the broken life that had been restored. His focus was not on her but on the potential that others would come with their issues and religious traditions he cherished would be replaced with a spiritual movement.

Now please hear me: Jesus did not set aside the Father's truth to fix a situation. Jesus never broke God's Law. He loved God's Word. He was defined by God's truth, and on a daily basis, He modeled the heart of God as it was clearly revealed through the revelations of God. Jesus was in a beautiful and intimate relationship with the Father and never had any allegiance to the rules of religion.

On this day, the official may have missed the miracle, but Jesus didn't miss his reaction. This official had his eyes so fixed on formality and rules of time-honored traditions that he lost sight of the incredible display of power right before his eyes. I can't imagine how this woman must have felt while still standing in front of everyone as her miracle of restoration was being condemned! In that moment, the Lion of Judah stepped in and spoke out, "Hypocrites! Doesn't each one of you untie his ox or donkey from the feeding trough on the Sabbath and lead it to water? Satan has bound this woman, a daughter of Abraham, for 18 years—shouldn't she be untied from this bondage on the Sabbath day?"

I love it! God's wisdom proved to be irrefutable compared to the rules of religion. But before we criticize this man, we need to remember that the church has been and still can be easily blinded by the rules of religion. The church has found that rules are clean and relationships are messy. Faith driven by rules is clean and can be easily followed. Here's my list of do's and here's my list of don'ts! And as much as we hate rules, we love rules. We love rules because rules lead us to the boundary, and we all want to know where our boundaries lie! Where's the edge? How far away from God can I wander and still be okay? How little do I need to do and still be covered by God's grace? But a relationship is different! Rules define the minimum, but relationships call for extravagance! You don't give the minimum in a relationship. If all you want to do is give the minimum in a relationship, then why be in the relationship? Relationships give us the opportunity to be extravagant! Our relationship with Jesus is founded on His extravagant love for us and is developed through our extravagant love for Him!

So what happened when rules met relationship? In verse 17 of this passage, we see opposing responses to what Jesus did that day. "When He had said these things, all His adversaries were humiliated, but the whole crowd was rejoicing over all the glorious things He was doing." Those who had bought into the rules were humiliated, but those who were open to a relationship with Jesus worshipped. People who define their salvation solely based on rules and rituals can become angry and inwardly focused. They believe their salvation is limited to being all about them. When I surrendered my life to Jesus Christ, I discovered that my salvation was bigger than my salvation!

Here's what I mean: God's grace made me free from the penalty of sin and granted me the right to approach the heavenly Father as a child of God, giving me both freedoms and responsibilities. Our salvation is so much bigger than just our salvation. We must celebrate our freedom while understanding that pride is what causes us to mistake the freedom to take pleasure in Christ with the freedom to take pleasure in sinful activities.

I love my God more than I love my freedoms. Jesus is not my homeboy. He is not my copilot. He is my God. I will bow before Him and humble myself in His presence, not in the presence of religion, but in Him alone. God chooses to lift me up and call me His child, but I will not allow that amazing gift—that amazing freedom—to produce pride and arrogance in my life. We must use our freedoms and rights for the purpose of seeing God's heart. God's Word is the best place to understand that journey.

Once Josiah heard God's Word and knew God's heart, it moved him. We have God's Word, but if we are not reading it and not taking the time to comprehend its truths, our lives are going to look a lot like Israel prior to Josiah finding a copy of the Scriptures. God's Word is a gift, but it is also a living necessity to all of us in Christ. Josiah found the knowledge of God and comprehended the truth—living truth that he allowed to change his life. He didn't try to create the will of God; he merely accepted it. He didn't look at how God's Word might affect his authority as king. Josiah wanted to be a slave to His God.

Look at how Josiah applied God's Word to His life:

> Then the king sent, and they gathered to him all the elders of Judah and of Jerusalem. The king went up to the house of the LORD and all the men of Judah and all the inhabitants of Jerusalem with him, and the priests and the prophets and all the people, both small and great; and he read in their hearing all the words of the book of the covenant which was found in the house of the LORD. The king stood by the pillar and made a covenant before the LORD, to walk after the LORD, and to keep His commandments and His testimonies and His statutes with all his heart and all his soul, to carry out the words of this covenant that were written in this book. And all the people entered into the covenant.
> —2 Kings 23:1–3 (NASU)

Josiah brought the people of Judah together, stood in front of them, and read God's Word. He went out to the edge of the temple and made a covenant to live by the knowledge of God's Word. Not only did he do it, but so did all the people with Him. You see, a covenant is a transformational relationship. You enter a covenant when you are saved, as you are transformed from death to life. You enter one when you are married, as you and your spouse become one flesh. Josiah entered a transformational relationship with God as he moved deeper into the will of God. He longed to live a life consistently surrendered to God.

On our journey deeper, as we pursue spiritual transformation into the image of Christ, I want each of us to recommit ourselves to a pursuit of the will of God through the Word of God. Please pray that the Holy Spirit will reveal to you the difference between the true commands of Scripture and the false rules of religion.

Our Covenant

I covenant before the Lord to walk after You, my Lord, and to keep Your commandments and Your testimonies and Your statutes with all my heart and all my soul, to carry out the words of this covenant as they are written in your Holy Word.

Study Questions

Intro video for group study can be found at
www.myjourneydeeper.com

1. Discuss the author's definition for the characteristic of knowledge: knowledge is the truth of God properly comprehended and applied.

2. Does the church have a proper view of biblical knowledge?

3. What impresses you about Josiah's love for God and His Word?

4. Why is spiritual apathy and biblical heresy such a dangerous issue for people of faith?

5. How do we balance our spiritual freedoms with biblical obedience?

6. What did you learn from this chapter and how can you apply it to your life?

7. What areas do you need to pray about or improve in your walk with Jesus?

Chapter 4
Training Kicks In

Step 1: Moral excellence is the God-given ability to perform heroic deeds.

Step 2: Knowledge is the truth of God properly comprehended and applied.

add to your faith
Self-Control

On a gorgeous Southern fall weekend, I decided to head home from college to get in a diving trip. I had begun dating my future wife, Lori, and thought this might be a great weekend to see her and my family and get some time on the water. On Saturday morning, we got ready for the dive, and since I was coming in from college, I needed to borrow some equipment. I was going to need a tank and set of regulators to breathe through. So after a few phone calls, I rounded up all the equipment I needed to make the dive.

As Todd, Lori, and I were heading out to our dive site, we were having a great time and got caught up in the beauty of the day. Once we arrived at the site, Lori made herself comfortable on the boat with a book while Todd and I began our dive. Once we settled at the bottom, I checked my gauges to confirm my air pressure and how much time we'd have at the bottom. My numbers were a little off, but I thought it must have been my excitement for the dive. I focused my breathing and continued to enjoy our time at the bottom. We were diving fifty to sixty feet down when I checked my gauges again and noticed that I was using more air than I should. I continued to tell myself to relax and breathe normally. I knew my rapid breathing had shortened my time on the bottom, but I still had time to play.

Todd and I were watching fish off a small man-made reef, and I was loving the day. I had begun following this small school of fish when all of a sudden I breathed in and got nothing. I looked at my gauges and found myself completely without air. I looked up and realized I wouldn't make it to the top without causing serious damage to my body. I began fin-kicking over toward Todd and signaled him that I was out of air by drawing an imaginary knife across my throat. Todd quickly handed me his spare regulator and we buddy breathed back to the surface. I couldn't believe I was out of air and couldn't figure out why I had used so much air on this dive. Once we were back safely in the boat and I was able to calm Lori down after the incident, we began to check the equipment and found a hole in the regulator hose. We had gotten so caught up in the excitement of the day that we forgot to take care of what was most essential: checking the equipment. Being properly trained not to panic and to maintain self-control is what ultimately prevented the day from being a total disaster.

Many times in life, just like that day I ran out of air sixty feet under, the difference between disaster and success is self-control. Executives, athletes, artists, and leaders—it doesn't matter what field you play on; there are a few things everyone needs to stay on task and avoid the pitfalls of mediocrity. Here are some questions to help clarify the journey and identify the distractions:

First, can you clearly state what prize you are pursuing?

Second, can you clearly state the goal (or goals) you have set to help you achieve your prize?

Third, have you planned a course of action to achieve your goal to win the prize?

Last, are you motivated enough to commit to the plan, especially when your desires conflict with the plan?

As we continue our journey through our focal passage (2 Peter 1:4–8), each chapter adds another layer to our transformation into the image of Christ. I pray that as you read these pages, you are feeding your faith and finding nourishment for your soul.

Step 3: Self-control is the restraint to trust the will of God over the will of self.

Now we are moving into an area of spiritual transformation that is somewhat scary to believers and completely foreign to nonbelievers. Self-control literally means "holding oneself in." In Peter's day, it would have been used to describe an athlete who was self-disciplined to look past the desires of the moment for a greater prize in the future.

> Do you not know that those who run in a race all run, but only one receives the prize? Run in such a way that you may win. Everyone who competes in the games exercises self-control in all things. They then do it to receive a perishable wreath, but we are imperishable.
> —1 Corinthians 9:24–25 (NASU)

Therefore, self-control defined for a follower of Christ is the restraint to trust the will of God over the will of self. Spiritually, self-control is part of the plan to become conformed to the image of Christ.

Let me show you what Peter, in our text, is challenging us to do on this journey of spiritual transformation. Basically, the discipline of self-control reveals our trust in the lordship of Jesus versus our desire for self-preservation. Trusting the Word of God and the spiritual direction of the Holy Spirit is more than participating in Christian activities. It is heartbreaking to realize how many people in the church trust Jesus with their salvation but refuse to trust Him with their daily lives. Somewhere along the way, these people realized they cannot control their eternal outcome, the whole heaven vs. hell decision of eternity, so they accepted God's invitation for eternity; however, they refuse to believe that God has a better grasp about how they ought to live out their daily lives.

Self-control is the restraint to trust the will of God over the will of self.

Though no one would say it out loud, many have stated with their lives, "God, I want the heaven thing, but life's too complicated to give You complete obedience." Have you ever used this statement: "It's easier to ask for forgiveness than to get permission"? I have. When I was growing up, it was my go-to thought every time I needed to make a questionable decision. Any time I wanted to do something I knew my parents would object to, I just did it and later asked them to forgive me. I hoped that pleading ignorance would help my case, but it never did.

Now, here's the big question: have you ever used it in your relationship with Christ? Have you ever justified an action you know you didn't pray about? You know God called you to do something else, but you disobeyed anyway, knowing all along you could clear your conscience with three little words: "Forgive me, God."

Don't be embarrassed. You are not the first to do it. The Galatians did it too, which prompted Paul to write a letter. He didn't mince words when he said, "Do not be deceived, God is not mocked; for whatever a man sows, this he will also reap" (Galatians 6:7 NASU). Paul wanted the church in Galatia to fully understand the difference between saying words you do not mean and repentance. Merely saying, "God forgive me," and asking God for His forgiveness from a repentant heart are two different acts. There are no magic words or spiritual loopholes to pursuing Christ and seeking forgiveness for our sins. The thought is *I've heard people say I cannot lose my salvation, so since God will do what He says and take me after I recited a prayer, then I'll do what I want, knowing that God has to keep His word even if I don't keep my word to Him.*

Yes, God is greater than us and His promises are perfect. Yes, He will always keep His word, and confession is necessary because Christians still sin. We will sin, but a person with godly self-control trusts the will of God enough to live out that trust daily. That person does not look for spiritual loopholes or play the forgiveness card in an attempt to beat the spiritual system.

Rick Warren, senior pastor at Saddleback Community Church in California, said it this way in day 26 of *The Purpose Driven Life*:

> Every temptation is an opportunity to do good. On the path to spiritual maturity, even temptation becomes a stepping-stone rather than a stumbling block when you realize that it is just as much an occasion to do the right thing as it is to do the wrong thing. Temptation simply provides the choice. While temptation is Satan's primary weapon to destroy you, God wants to use it to develop you. Every time you choose to do good instead of sin, you are growing in the character of Christ.

Self-control is not analyzing the situation and choosing your best option; it's your acceptance of God's will as your only option.

God has an opinion about everything. In fact, *God wants you to know His will more than you want to know His will.* Do you believe that statement? God wants you to know His will more than you want to know His will. God wants the best for you, and the greatest gift God will ever give you is Himself. He will show you His path and reveal His will for your life. Our job is to live His will step by step, not to formulate alternatives for His consideration. We need to remember that we are not sinning merely by being tempted. It is through temptation itself that we have some of the greatest opportunities to be found faithful. Sin begins when we turn our hearts toward the desires of the temptation.

God wants you to know His will more than you want to know His will.

I want to tell you about a guy who had every opportunity to do right and said all the right things, but in the end, he thought he had earned the right to be disobedient to God. Solomon had it all and had all kinds of opportunities to reflect the glory of God, but he blew it. Solomon was king of Israel, and he had all the tools, physically and mentally; however, God had some specific commands for the kings of Israel. I want to show a simple command given to the kings: "He shall not multiply wives for himself, or else his heart will turn away" (Deuteronomy 17:17 NASU).

That sounds clear and simple enough. As the king of God's people, Solomon was to demonstrate the intimacy and exclusivity of biblical marriage. Even if all the other kings had multiple wives, which served as a status symbol, God wanted the king of His people to be monogamous. As a young man, Solomon found a wife that he loved with all his heart. While building his house and the temple, he married Pharaoh's daughter. (See 1 Kings 3:1–3.) Things were going great for Solomon. Look at this conversation between God and Solomon: "At Gibeon the Lord appeared to Solomon in a dream at night. God said, 'Ask. What should I give you?'" (1 Kings 3:5 HCSB).

If God gave you one wish, what would you wish for? Would you use it on something huge like world peace or providing clean water to all third-world nations? Would you be tempted to use it on something personal like money or fame? God granted Solomon one request, one desire from his heart. What an amazing gift and equally incredible responsibility to have on your shoulders. Solomon took this moment to recognize his need for God.

> "Lord my God, You have now made Your servant king in my father David's place. Yet I am just a youth with no experience in leadership. Your servant is among Your people You have chosen, a people too numerous to be numbered or counted. So give Your servant an obedient heart to judge Your people and to discern between good and evil. For who is able to judge this great people of Yours?"
> —1 Kings 3:7–9 (HCSB)

Solomon did a remarkable thing. He asked to know God better and be able to discern good from evil. God loved Solomon's request and granted his desire plus so much more; however, as Solomon's power and popularity grew, he no longer sought God's wisdom. He trusted in his own. He began to believe he could handle the consequences of breaking the commands of God.

Have you ever weighed the consequences of obedience versus the consequences of sin and concluded that the sinful consequences were acceptable? It has become a common practice among believers, except we forget to weigh in the cost of breaking the heart of God. We look at the physical consequences, the earthly cost that might come back and bite us, but we avoid considering God's heart and how our sins wound the relationship He wants with us. We come back to the loophole of asking for God to forgive us without any desire for repentance.

In addition to misplaced trust and a lack of repentance, Solomon had another problem. Women! He wanted them. His flesh wanted them, and Solomon was brought to a moment of decision. He had to choose between demonstrating self-control and loving his wife or pursuing the desires of his flesh. In the end, Solomon had rationalized that military alliances through marriage to many different women were of greater strategic value than the will of God. He justified his actions.

The spiritual transformation of self-control is not found in our ability to sin and clear our conscience through public displays of corporate worship but in our ability to accept God's plan and live by it. Just because humanity desires to downplay our sin, nothing in the nature of God allows Him to take the same light view of our sin. As followers of Christ, we need to be wounded by those things that wound God.

If you think Solomon's problem was inconsequential, take a look at the following passage:

> Now King Solomon loved many foreign women along with the daughter of Pharaoh: Moabite, Ammonite, Edomite, Sidonian, and Hittite women, from the nations concerning which the LORD had said to the sons of Israel, "You shall not associate with them, nor shall they associate with you, for they will surely turn your heart away after their gods." Solomon held fast to these in love. He had seven hundred wives, princesses, and three hundred concubines, and his wives turned his heart away. For when Solomon was old, his wives turned his heart away after other gods; and his heart was not wholly devoted to the LORD his God, as the heart of David his father had been.
> —1 Kings 11:1–4 (NASU)

Solomon's spiritual journey gives us a compelling example of what it means to trust God and then to forsake that trust. Early in his life, God granted him anything he wanted, and all he wanted was God. Later in his life, Solomon became convinced of his own sufficiency. He may have worshiped the one true God, but he also worshiped the pagan gods brought to him by his wives. Solomon did what was evil in the sight of the LORD, and did not follow the LORD fully, as David his father had done (1 Kings 11:1–6 NASU).

Solomon missed it, and his life gives us an honest picture of a man without self-control. But what does it look like when someone does it right? In Genesis 37, Joseph was sold into slavery by his brothers;

however, Joseph's journey would not end with him a slave. Due to a series of God-driven encounters where Joseph demonstrated amazing self-control and honorable character, he eventually was elevated to a place where he could do great harm to his brothers. One day they would stand before him completely at his mercy. Joseph would one day have the opportunity to grant life or sentence death to the brothers who betrayed him.

Joseph was a man who found himself dishonored, wounded, abandoned, and rejected by his brothers, but the biblical account of Joseph provides a great example of one who understood the power of self-control. We see it demonstrated when he fled temptation the day he was approached by his master's wife. Joseph started as a young man torn from his home and sold into slavery, but he distinguished himself in his duties and found himself elevated to a high position in his master's house. When approached by his master's wife about having an affair, Joseph fled from the situation. He didn't try to justify his actions; he accepted God's Word on the subject and separated himself from the sin. Joseph's actions, however, were not met with praise but with a prison. Thrown into jail for doing the right thing, Joseph had to once again face the decision about how he would deal with unjust treatment. Once again faced with the rollercoaster journey of his life, Joseph did not abandon the character that he knew would honor God.

> The warden did not bother with anything under Joseph's authority, because the Lord was with him, and the Lord made everything that he did successful (Genesis 39:23 HCSB).

During the time Joseph was spending in jail, he interpreted dreams for royal prisoners informing one of his death and the other of his release. Years later, after no one could interpret a dream for Pharaoh, the royal cupbearer remembered Joseph. God granted Joseph the wisdom to interpret Pharaoh's dream, and he immediately gave all the glory to God. Amazed by Joseph's wisdom, Pharaoh gave Joseph a new position, making him the second most powerful man in Egypt with the authority to do great harm to anyone. Pharaoh's dream had revealed a famine in the land, leaving people from all over coming to Egypt seeking to buy food. Among the foreigners entering Egypt to buy food were Joseph's brothers. Finally, after all these years, Joseph could get revenge. Yet with all the power and with no fear of consequences, Joseph didn't seek revenge. He showed mercy and self-control.

> Then Joseph said to his brothers, "Please, come near me," and they came near. "I am Joseph, your brother," he said, "the one you sold into Egypt. And now don't be worried or angry with yourselves for selling me here, because God sent me ahead of you to preserve life."
> —Genesis 45:4–5 (HCSB)

Joseph had been hurt deeply by his brothers. Abandoned and alone, he knew great pain, lasting pain; however, Joseph was able to show the self-control to forgive and honor the very men who hurt him! How? I believe Joseph could see God's blessings in other areas of his life which allowed Him to see God's hand clear enough to forgive his brothers. Joseph didn't compartmentalize his life. He didn't see the blessings over in one box and the pains in another box. He didn't credit God with the blessings and his brothers with the pain. He knew God was over his whole life and, therefore, he honored others, even those who hurt him. He lived a life of self-control.

Joseph personally honored those who had dishonored him. But what about us? What do we do if we also struggle with personally dishonoring others just because we feel we have the right to do so? These times represent a lack of self-control based on our character, not their actions. This one is tough to admit and takes a supernatural amount of humility to see this character in our lives. In fact, you cannot see it unless God reveals it. Others can see it in you and me, but without God, we won't see it in ourselves.

In these relationships, many times we don't show self-control because we feel small. We unconsciously need more glory and more personal recognition and, therefore, are unwilling to forgive others or esteem someone else. Self-control looks like weakness, yet God takes a very different approach to self-control. "For everyone who exalts himself will be humbled, and the one who humbles himself will be exalted" (Luke 14:11 HCSB). Men and women with self-control are content with who they are in Christ, even as they grow and develop to do greater things. They don't need to exalt themselves, while small people who desperately desire to be exalted are afraid of showing self-control because they believe it pushes the other guy forward and diminishes their own glory. Self-control helps us stay focused on God in the midst of our greatest temptations.

Paul addressed this temptation with the young pastor, Timothy.

- "But flee from these things, you man of God, and pursue righteousness, godliness, faith, love, perseverance and gentleness" (1 Timothy 6:11 NASU).

- "Now flee from youthful lusts and pursue righteousness, faith, love and peace, with those who call on the Lord from a pure heart" (2 Timothy 2:22 NASU).

Remember what we stated earlier in the book: confession is a sign of spiritual strength, not spiritual weakness. Self-control is built on the confessions of people who are more concerned about conforming to the image of Christ than protecting a false image of spirituality. Joseph remembered and Solomon forgot: your spiritual reputation in the community might be formed by sporadic religious deeds from your past, but your spiritual transformation is forged every day by your decisions to trust and live the will of God.

One of the key tools to continual transformation is accountability, which is nothing more than a true partnership of restoration. Accountability involves intentional friendships that grow into spiritual partnerships for the purpose of seeing each other grow into the image of Christ. It's a safe place between two people who want to see each other succeed spiritually. Are you vulnerable enough to let someone else into your life to help you on this journey? Are you willing to personally sacrifice time, energy, and resources to see someone else grow closer to the image of Christ? It's a journey meant to be done in community. Yet what we've discovered is that God's heart toward others is unnatural to the human nature. The natural response of the human nature is passivity or pride. In other words, "If I have excess time or resources, I'll consider my options and see if I think God's heart is worth my sacrifice." It's easy to say, "My faith is private," and avoid accountability, but faith was always meant to be personal, not private.

Exhibiting self-control is a battle, and inside each and every one of us, our preference and our mission are at war in every decision. The passivity of not getting involved is at war with the mission of our lives. It's easy to know but hard to accept that all of us are called to get involved somewhere! We cannot overstate or underestimate the priority God places on loving one another. "For the entire law is fulfilled in one statement: You shall love your neighbor as yourself" (Galatians 5:14 HCSB).

A few verses later, Paul would help define what it means to love others. "Carry one another's burdens; in this way you will fulfill the law of Christ" (Galatians 6:2 HCSB). The true burden of the Christian faith is not laws defining do's and don'ts; the true burden of the Christian faith is the responsibility we have to others.

One of the foundational keys to the church being the church is found in the power of circles—groups of believers who celebrate when others celebrate and weep when others weep. The early church functioned in home groups, or small groups gathered together, to pray together, study together, and minister together and to each other. When Jesus took his small group to an upper room, they prayed together, they worshipped together, they learned together, and they got honest with each other. Then Jesus reminded them that being together is not enough. They must serve each other. So he knelt before them and washed their feet.

> When Jesus had washed their feet and put on His robe, He reclined again and said to them, "Do you know what I have done for you? You call Me Teacher and Lord. This is well said, for I am. So if I, your Lord and Teacher, have washed your feet, you also ought to wash one another's feet. For I have given you an example that you also should do just as I have done for you.
> —John 13:12–15 (HCSB)

Discipleship teaches and helps meet needs.

Prayer covers us and helps meet needs.

Fellowship deepens relationships and helps meet needs.

Evangelism reaches others who are hurting and helps meet needs.

Accountability develops trust and helps meet needs.

Ministry shows the love of Christ and helps meet needs.

The heart of every small group is to wash each other's feet.

I know connecting to a small group can be one of the scariest things to do in your spiritual life, but like so many other steps of faith, it's one we need to do for God's glory and the benefit of others. The scariest day I ever had diving was that day I ran out of air. If I had been diving alone or unwilling to use my buddy, I'd be dead or, at the very least, damaged. A dive buddy is essential to safety and dealing with the dangers of diving; it is the perfect picture of accountability. You never want to dive alone. There are always unforeseen dangers in diving, and there are countless dangers in life. Accountability, whether in groups or individually, provides the buddy system needed to survive.

Self-control is the restraint to trust the will of God over the will of self. It is a daily battle and, if done alone, can feel impossible. Most people do not intentionally or blatantly abandon their pursuit of the image of Christ; instead, they spiritually justify their actions and try to have it all. Yet we can't have it all. Salvation is an exchange, and in every exchange, something is surrendered or sacrificed for something else to be gained. The value of what is gained is based on the value of what is being sacrificed. Do you want to understand just how much God loves you? *Our value is not determined by the world's opinion of us but in what God exchanged for us.*

God, the Father, sent Jesus to exchange the expanses of heaven and the adoration of being God for the restrictions of flesh and the rejections of His own creation. Why? Because God loves you! The Father sent the Son in exchange for an opportunity to be in a relationship with you! A Father willing to sacrifice His Son. A Son willing to humble Himself even to the point of death on a cross. The Holy Spirit living inside His own creation. The magnitude of the exchange is beyond what we can fully understand, but it is worth the sacrifice of self-control.

---

*Our value is not determined by the world's opinion
of us but in what God exchanged for us.*

Study Questions

Intro video for group study can be found at
www.myjourneydeeper.com

1. Discuss the author's definition for the characteristic of self-control: self-control is the restraint to trust the will of God over the will of self.

2. Can you clearly state what prize you are pursuing with your faith?

   • Can you clearly state the goal (or goals) you have set to help you achieve your prize?

   • Have you planned a course of action to achieve your goal to win the prize?

   • Are you motivated enough to commit to the plan, especially when your desires conflict with the plan?

3. Why do we have a hard time believing God wants us to know His will more than we want to know His will?

4. What do you see as key differences in the lives of Solomon and Joseph?

5. How important is it for individuals in the church to have a heart for others?

6. What did you learn from this chapter, and how can you apply it to your life?

7. What areas do you need to pray about or improve in your walk with Jesus?

Chapter 5
The Battle

Step 1: Moral excellence is the God-given ability to perform heroic deeds.

Step 2: Knowledge is the truth of God properly comprehended and applied.

Step 3: Self-control is the restraint to trust the will of God over the will of self.

add to your faith
Perseverance

One of reasons I wanted to learn how to dive was to catch lobsters. I had heard Todd and Andy tell stories of diving for lobsters in the Florida Keys, and I wanted to be part of those dives. A short time after I had begun diving, Dr. Mignerey asked me if I wanted to go lobster diving with him and the boys. I was so excited, but I couldn't figure out how we were going to get away to the Keys. Dr. Mignerey explained to me that there were lobsters off the northern coast of the Gulf of Mexico, and we could go out the next weekend.

I couldn't wait to finally go lobster diving, but I still doubted Dr. Mignerey's story. What kind of lobsters were living in the gulf? I was a little afraid that I was being sent on a "snipe hunt." Saturday rolled around, and we were on the way out to our dive site. As we prepped for the dive, I was being told that we'd be diving in water more than one hundred feet deep, which would push us past our no-decompression limits and force us to limit the amount of time we could spend on the bottom. At deeper levels, nitrogen builds up in a diver's body, making it necessary for the divers to factor in time to decompress.

Never having been on a lobster dive before, I wasn't a hundred percent sure how this worked, and now I would be factoring in the limited time and depth of the dive. Once we were over the site, I was handed a broken fishing pole and a net that is normally used to pull fish into the boat.

"What are these for?" I asked Todd.

"The pole is to tickle the lobster, and once he comes out of his hole, we spook him backward into the net."

Well, then, I knew I was getting played! Or so I thought. Dr. Mignerey really started giving me lessons on how to tickle a lobster. I thought they were crazy, but I was beginning to believe that we were really going after lobsters by tickling them. Crazy or not, I was getting excited about the possibilities of going on my first lobster dive. Todd and I started to the bottom and began looking for our first catch but found nothing. We only had about ten minutes on the bottom, and as our time clicked away, I couldn't believe that my first dive for lobsters was going to be a bust. Looking at my watch and noticing that we were on our last minute, I paddled over to Todd. I was ready to start up.

As we moved back toward the anchor line, Todd hit my arm and pointed to a rock formation to our left. I finally saw the lobster's head between the rocks. Todd handed me the net, and he began to tickle the lobster. Knowing time was very limited, Todd repeatedly tried to get the lobster out of his hole so I could put the net behind him. But after a minute and no luck, we knew it was time to go to the top. Todd's efforts, however, had revealed that this was a huge lobster, and we couldn't bring ourselves to leave it. He handed me all the equipment, put his feet on the rocks, grabbed the lobster by the antennas (gulf lobsters don't have claws), and pulled him out of the hole and onto his chest.

Once out of the hole, Todd bear-hugged the lobster, and we started to the decompression line. We knew we had to spend a few minutes on the line due to the time and depth at which we had been diving. It wasn't until we had gotten to the decompression mark that we realized this lobster was truly massive. Later, we weighed him at more than six and a half pounds! We had stretched our time on bottom and tried multiple ways to catch the lobster. I had been ready to quit, but Todd couldn't. He was going to fight and finish the task. The lobster we found that day wasn't just another lobster; it was the largest one they had ever caught.

In life, there are battles we should walk away from. There are also battles too special, too important, to abandon. Just like Todd's battle for the lobster, the battle for faith in our culture is worth fighting again and again. Generations ago, faith and culture were entwined, and it was hard to tell the difference between faith and cultural conformity to a belief in God. Today, culture and faith are going in opposite directions like bullets from dueling guns.

Years have passed since the incident at Columbine High School in Colorado, but the legacy of those who lost their lives still resonates as a call to persevere in our faith. On April 20, 1999, sixteen-year-old Cassie Bernall handed her friend Amanda Meyer a note that said, "Honestly, I totally want to live my life completely for God. It's hard and scary, but totally worth it!" Later that day, she was shot to death for her faith by a gunman who asked, "Do you believe in God?"

Rachel Scott was also among those killed. One year earlier, she had written in her diary, "I'm not going to apologize for speaking the name of Jesus. I'm not going to hide the light God has put in me. If I have to sacrifice everything, I will." And she did. What brought Cassie and Rachel to that place of total abandonment was perseverance, and that is the next quality we add to our faith.

Step 4: Perseverance is the spiritual staying power that gives believers the courage to literally die instead of rejecting the faith.

That sounds a lot like self-control, doesn't it? What is the difference between self-control and perseverance? Self-control has to do with handling the *pleasures* of life, while perseverance is a victorious endurance through the *pressures* and *problems* of life. We always learn from looking at the original language. The Greek word for *perseverance* (some translations use *patience*) is *hupomone*, pronounced hoopomonay. It means "cheerful (or hopeful) endurance" or "constancy."

Perseverance is the spiritual staying power that gives believers the courage to literally die instead of rejecting the faith.

It's the same word Paul uses in Romans 5:3–5.

> Not only so, but we also rejoice in our sufferings, because we know that suffering produces perseverance; perseverance, character; and character, hope. And hope does not disappoint us, because God has poured out his love into our hearts by the Holy Spirit, whom he has given us.
> —Romans 5:3–5 9 (NIV)

How many of us can "rejoice in our sufferings"? Paul is telling the young persecuted believers in Rome to view their trials as a path to hope. Paul believes that when suffering and endurance are surrendered to the conviction that God is in control, then each of us can know that God is walking with us and teaching us through these moments for a greater purpose and for His eternal glory. The picture Paul is painting for us in Romans is one of the disciplines needed to follow a conviction even when everything in your own flesh and will wants to rebel against it. This is truly one of the most challenging steps on the journey to reflecting the image of Christ.

What do we mean when we say we have conviction? Having a conviction is to be thoroughly convinced that something is absolutely true and something for which you will take a stand, regardless of the consequences. Now the truth that we have to wrestle with is this: is there a difference between belief and conviction?

The rich, young ruler discovered the difference in belief and conviction when he came to Jesus and asked which beliefs are important, to which Jesus responded with all the requirements the young man had probably been taught all his life. He said, "I'm doing all these things." Jesus, in essence, then said, "Okay, son, let's add conviction to your beliefs."

"If you want to be perfect," Jesus said to him, "go, sell your belongings and give to the poor, and you will have treasure in heaven. Then come, follow Me" (Matthew 19:21 HCSB).

Conviction takes belief one step farther. Today, it seems that we believe so much and are convicted by so little. Paul had great beliefs that became his convictions, and he lived out those convictions. He suffered greatly for his beliefs and convictions.

> Five times I received from the Jews 40 lashes minus one. Three times I was beaten with rods. Once I was stoned. Three times I was shipwrecked. I have spent a night and a day in the depths of the sea. On frequent journeys, I faced dangers from rivers, dangers from robbers, dangers from my own people, dangers from the Gentiles, dangers in the city, dangers in the open country, dangers on the sea, and dangers among false brothers; labor and hardship, many sleepless

nights, hunger and thirst, often without food, cold, and lacking clothing. Not to mention other things, there is the daily pressure on me: my care for all the churches.
—2 Corinthians 11:24–28 (NIV)

Even through all this physical hardship, Paul's focus was not on his suffering but on his investment to these churches. Paul could live out his convictions because of his hope in the power and glory of a greater God.

For this reason I also suffer these things, but I am not ashamed; for I know whom I have believed and I am convinced (convicted) *that He is able to guard what I have entrusted to Him until that day.*
—2 Timothy 1:12 (NASU)

Cassie Bernall and Rachel Scott had moved beyond beliefs to conviction. They had investigated and accepted the truth of Jesus and allowed those beliefs to become the convictions which drove their actions. They were passionate for God.

There is a reason why Scripture tells us to add knowledge to our faith before we add the conviction of perseverance.

I'll give you an example I read from Bruce Carter, on www.valleyviewseek.org/value-faith.

One evening, nineteen men read a prayer-laden letter regarding their last night on earth. It said,

Be obedient on this night because you will be facing situations that are the ultimate and that would not be done except with full obedience. When you engage in the battle, strike as heroes would strike. As god says, strike above the neck and strike from everywhere and then you will know all the heavens are decorated in the best way to meet you.

The next morning, September 11, 2001, those nineteen men gave their lives for what they believed. Those terrorists had deep convictions and, from their point of view, were serving a just and holy war. They are a vivid reminder that people can have deep convictions and still be tragically wrong. Wrong beliefs produce tragic convictions. So as we begin adding perseverance to our faith, we need to put handles around a couple of pieces of truth. I hope this truth will drive you to conviction.

First, perseverance is built on your trust in your beliefs. Paul persevered through all his trials because he was so convinced of his beliefs.

> For this reason I also suffer these things, but I am not ashamed; for I know whom I have believed and I am convinced that He is able to guard what I have entrusted to Him until that day.
> —2 Timothy 1:12 (NASU)

The world is calling believers to a greater point of decision. Do I believe what I say I believe? And will I allow it to affect my life?

Second, persevered convictions must come from investigated truth. We don't need to wonder, we need to examine God's Word to substantiate what we think we believe. That's when belief becomes conviction that results in perseverance. Before you believe something blindly, investigate and reason out the natural conclusion of this belief.

> For everything that was written in the past was written to teach us, so that through endurance and the encouragement of the Scriptures we might have hope.
> —Romans 15:4 (NIV)

Imagine that you're at a Christian conference and one of the speakers gets up and says, "Our faith is founded on the Word of God!" You, along with everyone else, start screaming, "Amen!" Then an hour later, another speaker gets up and says, "Our faith is built on the church, the bride of Christ!" and again, everybody starts screaming, "Amen!" The problem is these statements are mutually exclusive of one another. Are we just splitting hairs? No, the illustration I just gave you started the Reformation and divided Martin Luther from the Roman Catholic Church, costing thousands of lives.

Study, investigate, question, and let revealed truth move you from beliefs to the convictions worthy of your life. You may be asking, "Is this safe? I mean, I agree we need to be a more moral people, and we need to help the needy, but you're talking about convictions like you're willing to bank your life on them."

Is being a Christ follower—that is, willing to strive for moral excellence, bound to the truth of God, surrendered to His authority, and committed to persevere through the trials of life—safe? No! God has not called us to a life filled with guarantees of money and great health. In fact, He has called us to live a life beyond ourselves. Every day when we're faced with the consequences of life, we begin to feel the pressure of life closing in on us. The pressures and problems of life often make us want to close our hearts to living a dangerous life. The most dangerous decision we will ever make is to give God control of our lives. Not because He will call us to give up our lives for His glory but just the opposite—because He will ask us to live every day for His glory. In order to persevere, we must discipline ourselves to open wide our hearts to God. "Trust in the Lord with all your heart and do not lean on your own understanding. In all your ways acknowledge Him, And He will make your paths straight" (Proverbs 3:5–6 NASU).

> "Is he safe?" the children ask.
> "Safe?" said Mr. Beaver. "Who said anything about safe? Course he isn't safe, but he's good. He's the king, I tell you."
> —C. S. Lewis, *The Lion, the Witch, and the Wardrobe*

Jesus is not safe. He is not manageable. He is a wild lion. He is not safe, but he is good. When you persevere, you reflect the character of the King. What happens when the destination we want is out of reach? What happens when we make the right decision in one area and it leads to peace in that situation, but we find ourselves struck down in a different area of our lives?

A young person may be committed to saving themselves physically until marriage and expect to date wonderful people who will honor that decision. What if their dates don't support that decision, or what if they can't seem to get a date because of their reputation for purity? Where's the reward?

A businessman shoots straight with his finances when it seems like everyone in the industry bumps their numbers to appease management. He expects his honesty to be appreciated by the company, but he is overlooked for bonuses and promotions. He's still pleased with his honesty until he discovers that he has a serious medical issue. This is not what he expected in return.

What happens when we become one of those stories? What happens when we've worked toward a particular destination, we've made the right decisions, yet we can never achieve the goal? We're unable to have the dream job or the dream house, or we're unable to experience the desired picture for family, perhaps due to a wayward child or the loss of a child.

The truth is that disappointments can drive us into some harsh cycles. A rebellious teen can drive wedges into a marriage. The desire for love can move someone into a relationship that doesn't end in marriage but with wounds they will carry for the rest of their life. The loss of a job can leave you depressed and distant from those who still need you. Many people at some point in their life have screamed to God, "I'm not where I want to be! This isn't the picture I had for my life!" But we're here now, so what do we do?

One of the reasons I love Scripture is the honesty it brings to the lives of those we find in its pages. Not just the stories where the heroes celebrate another victory, but where heroes also walk through loss and must forsake the picture of their perfect destination.

One of the clearest examples of an unexpected ending was King David's story. All the Kings of Israel and Judah were compared to King David. When Rehoboam, David's grandson, became King, he was unwilling to seek or receive wise counsel. The kingdom was divided, and Jeroboam, an accomplished leader for the people, took the Northern Kingdom. A remnant, however, was left to Rehoboam because of David's faithfulness to God. David made right decisions, and God recognized those decisions and urged others to follow his example. Looking forward to the later years of David's life, we don't see a man enjoying God's blessings; we see a man struggling to keep his life from falling apart. David's life was not turning out like he pictured; when he should have been enjoying his grown kids and playing with his grandkids, he found his life spiraling out of control. David's story fleshes out one of our key nuggets for this chapter: Once I accept that the crisis over me is under God, I can endure it and even glorify God in the journey.

David's life was about to completely unravel, and he never saw it coming. David's firstborn son and heir to the throne was named Amnon. Unfortunately, Amnon faced a despicable issue; he loved his half-sister, Tamar. Cultural views on this have not changed, and just like today, that kind of relationship was unacceptable and illegal. But Amnon didn't care, and scripture tells us that he became infatuated with his sister. In the depravity of his heart, He devised a plan to be alone with his sister by pretending to be sick and asking her to feed him. Before the night was over, he restrained her and begged her to be with him. Tamar pleaded with him to let her go, but no matter how much she resisted, he raped her. Thankfully, it didn't take long for the news to reach the king's ear.

King David was outraged! As angry as he was, however, the King did nothing! But that's His daughter! Why? How? How could he let that go? Maybe it was because Amnon was next in line for the throne, and he didn't want this out in front of the people. Maybe fear and guilt of his past sins with Bathsheba and Uriah's murder left him paralyzed and disqualified to react to the issue. Whatever the reason, he did nothing. David had a lifetime of wisdom, but it was useless in this moment. His failure to act set off a series of events that forever altered his future.

Tamar went to another family member, her brother, Absalom, but this time, she found the protection she needed and the revenge she wanted. Absalom was the son most like David as a young and passionate king. His rage did not lead him to act quickly, but, instead, he waited two years to find the perfect moment to take revenge. Absalom threw a party for all his brothers and sisters, and when they were relaxed, his men entered the hall and murdered Amnon. Once he had avenged his sister, he fled to another country.

Upon hearing about the murder, David once again was broken; one son had just murdered another son. David knew he should hunt Absalom down and punish him for stepping in and taking justice into his own hands, but again, David did nothing. His world was falling apart. David was a man so honored by God that God divided the kingdom to keep a remnant of Israel under the rule of his family... a man so honored by God that his family line would bring us to the Messiah, our Savior Jesus. Yet David's life was a disaster.

Push the story forward three years, and we learn that David began to miss his son. David's general, Joab, organized for Absalom to reenter the country and move back to Jerusalem, but with one restriction. David declared that Absalom could return to his house, "but he may not see my face" (2 Samuel 14:24 HCSB). Absalom was confused by this restriction and called for Joab to explain what was going on, but Joab ignored his request. Absalom had Joab's field burned to get his attention. When Joab confronted him about the fire, Absalom demanded to see his father, and a meeting was arranged.

> Joab went to the king and told him. So David summoned Absalom, who came to the king and bowed down before him with his face to the ground. Then the king kissed Absalom.
> —2 Samuel 14:33 (HCSB)

A quick, ceremonial kiss was all he got. It recognized his return but also that nothing else would be offered in the relationship. Absalom never forgave his father, and for the next four years, he planned and he waited. At every turn we see that Absalom was a patient but proactive man. So over those four years, he sat at the city gate and redirected situations being brought to the king to himself. In doing so, he "stole the hearts of the men of Israel" (2 Samuel 15:6 HCSB). At the end of four years, Absalom went to Hebron and had himself proclaimed king of Israel. David's inactivity at home was now tearing his nation in two.

As you can see, based on decisions made by other people, David's desired destination was lost forever. When David got the news, it was a dark day. Family tragedy had turned into a nation's new reality. It was the day when relentless arguing turns into divorce. The day of knowing your child is hanging out with the wrong crowd and getting the phone call about an incident. The news about Absalom's rebellion was that kind of day for David. When messengers reached David with the news, he was crushed. Defeated, he left Jerusalem with the people watching and weeping. David didn't want to fight his son. He didn't want to fight because the picture he had envisioned for his family was being completely destroyed and gone forever.

Once David got outside the city walls, however, Zadok, the high priest, ordered that the ark of the covenant be carried before David into any battle he would fight. In this critical moment, we see David's faith in God. David was in a place he never could have imagined. As we take a closer look at this, I want us to see the resolve of a faith deep enough to sustain a man who would never achieve the future he wanted.

> Then the king instructed Zadok, "Return the ark of God to the city. If I find favor in the Lord's eyes, He will bring me back and allow me to see both it and its dwelling place. However, if He should say, 'I do not

delight in you,' then here I am—He can do with me whatever pleases Him."
—2 Samuel 15:25–26 (HCSB)

I love Andy Stanley's conclusion of David's thought process in his book *The Principle of the Path* that says, "David realized that God can be trusted but not manipulated." David was not going to force God's hand by using the ark to fight his battle. David was not going to rely on any tangible thing from God, even the ark, to produce favorable results with the will of God. David's faith was not in the power of God's symbols to give him what he wanted. His faith was in God Himself! David trusted the will of God enough to reflect the character of God. In other words, David's faith was in a good, righteous, and holy God, and if God wanted to walk David through a storm, then David looked for God's will in the storm. The presence of the storm didn't bring David to the point where he questioned his faith or questioned the goodness of God. This moment of crisis brought David to the place where he leaned more on God. David's crisis was real; it was painful, and it hurt him deeply. David mourned his situation.

One day while David was on the run he climbed the slope of the Mount of Olives, weeping as he ascended. His head was covered, as a sign of brokenness and mourning. Each of the people with him covered their heads and went up, weeping as they ascended (2 Samuel 15:30 HCSB). David mourned, but finally, he turned and fought. He mourned his situation. He probably spent a significant amount of time seeking the Lord's face and asking for forgiveness for his sins in this situation. After a time of mourning and repentance he turned around and started to fight.

What's important to remember through all of this is, *when God forgives you, forgive yourself!* Take a second and get your mind wrapped around that idea. When God forgives you, forgive yourself! Don't keep dredging up the same sins. Let go of the guilt and, as David had prayed earlier in his life after repenting from his affair with Bathsheba and the murder of her husband, "restore the joy your salvation" (Psalm 51 HCSB).

When God forgives you, forgive yourself!

Guilt is a tool of Satan. Conviction is a tool of God. Guilt is broad and general and freezes us from moving forward. Conviction is specific and is only used to restore a person's relationship with God. David had been frozen but remembered the amazing freedom of grace, and it empowered him to do the work God had for him to do.

Absalom entered Jerusalem and sat on the throne, but as long as his father was on the run, the country would be divided. So Absalom pursued David and his army in the forest of Ephraim, where David's army ambushed Absalom's army. It was a rout. More than 20,000 men died in that single battle, but David ordered his men to bring Absalom to him alive. Joab, however, disobeyed David's command and took Absalom's life. We don't know why Joab disobeyed David. Maybe he knew that David just wanted this nightmare part of his life to end and Joab was afraid that he wouldn't punish Absalom. Perhaps he was sick after watching 20,000 men die that day. No matter what reason Joab had for killing Absalom, it was just another horrible chapter in David's story. You see, the general saw an insurrectionist; all David saw was his son.

Here we have one of the best known and most quoted lines from this passage:

> The king was deeply moved and went up to the gate chamber and wept. As he walked, he cried, "My son Absalom! My son, my son Absalom! If only I had died instead of you, Absalom, my son, my son!"
> —2 Samuel 18:33 (HCSB)

Remember David had stated, "He can do with me whatever pleases Him" (2 Samuel 15:26). Yet the pain was real, and he still wept over the results. David never fully understood why his family picture fell apart, yet one thousand years later, one of his descendants would kneel down close to this same spot and pray a similar prayer as He walked through a storm while saying, "Yet not my will, but yours be done" (Luke 22:42 NIV). Jesus knew the cross was not a storm he wanted to endure. To Jesus the greater victory was not in gaining the absence of the storm but was in knowing that He was in the center of God's will.

We need to ask ourselves this: is my primary destination the absence of the storm or the center of God's will?

What if we find out that the only place to find God's will is in the center of the storm?

Study Questions

Intro video for group study can be found at
www.myjourneydeeper.com

1. Discuss the author's definition for the characteristic of perseverance: perseverance is the spiritual staying power that gives believers the courage to literally die instead of rejecting the faith.

2. What are some similarities between spiritually navigating the distractions of pleasure and the pressures from our problems?

3. How does passivity destroy perseverance?

4. Why can't we forgive ourselves?

5. What did you learn from this chapter and how can you apply it to your life?

6. What areas do you need to pray about or improve in your walk with Jesus?

Chapter 6
Endless Treasure

Step 1: Moral excellence is the God-given ability to perform heroic deeds.

Step 2: Knowledge is the truth of God properly comprehended and applied.

Step 3: Self-control is the restraint to trust the will of God over the will of self.

Step 4: Perseverance is the spiritual staying power that gives believers the courage to literally die instead of rejecting the faith.

add to your faith
Godliness

One Saturday morning, Dr. Mignerey told Todd, Andy, and me that we were headed to dive a sunken wreck we had never seen. I was excited to dive a new site and experience a new wreck. Dr. Mignerey was describing the size of the wreck and the different things we'd see at the bottom. The more he talked, the more excited we became. But once we arrived at the site, the choppy water we saw slowed our fervent approach. The current only seemed to be getting stronger- we could barely see anything at all. Concerned for our safety on a new dive site, Dr. Mignerey had us waiting until the current began to settle. He soon realized that our time was getting cut short, and we could eventually waste the day waiting for a dive that might never happen. We reluctantly pulled up the anchor line. We were so disappointed that we couldn't make the dive.

Dr. Mignerey could sense our disappointment and told us, "Guys, I have an idea. It might take a little while to get to our new site, but trust me, it will be worth the effort and will more than salvage the day." After traveling miles across the gulf, we headed to the new site with an air of mystery about what we would experience once we got there. We eagerly dropped our line as we received all the necessary details, like ocean depth and time we could spend on the bottom. Then, much to our surprise, we were told to take a bag to the bottom. Now more curious than ever, I was really looking forward to seeing why we would need a bag for the bottom. We each flipped off the boat and made our way down to around fifty feet and began looking around for a wreck or a man-made reef. All we saw was sand and water.

Confused and kind of disappointed, we couldn't figure out why Dr. Mignerey thought this was such a cool site... until Andy pointed to the sand. We realized that we were diving in a bed of sand dollars! As far as we could see, there were sand dollars the size of pancakes. On the shore, you could spend years looking for a whole sand dollar the size of a silver dollar, but here were hundreds of huge, complete sand dollars covering the floor of the gulf. We spent the rest of our time filling our bags with the largest ones we could find before heading back to the surface. On the ride back, we compared our treasures, utterly amazed by what we had seen. One of the most amazing dives of my life started with being redirected away from where I wanted to go to a place where I had no idea what I was going to experience.

Often, our faith will take us on a journey with many of the same twists and turns. God desires to take us on an adventure full of mysterious experiences, and in our character journey, the next step is one of those mysteries. The next layer of transformation adds godliness to our lives. Godliness is a difficult word to define. If someone asks you, "What does godliness mean?" you might tell them, "It means to be godly."

"But what does *that* mean?"

"Well, I don't know. To be like God?"

Hang on. Isn't that what this whole study is about? If godliness is the pursuit of becoming like God, and this whole focal passage we're studying is about becoming like Christ, then why is it listed as one of the steps in the process? Shouldn't it read, "Add to your faith a pursuit of godliness, which includes moral excellence, knowledge, etc."? There has to be something there that God wants us to see. God's lesson on godliness is an eye opener. It takes us to a place we're not expecting.

Look back at 2 Peter 1:3 (NASU).

> His divine power has granted to us everything pertaining to life and **godliness,** through the true knowledge of Him who called us by His own glory and excellence.

In this verse, God gives us a difficult piece of truth. The way I believe God intended us to receive this truth is the same way I believe every customer should receive food- the way the cook prepared it. I waited tables in college, and I know that a good waiter doesn't look at the entrée and begin stirring things around, or look at the meal, evaluate the customer, believe the dish is too spicy, and go and scrape off the condiments. A good waiter brings the meal to the table as close as possible to the way the chef prepared it.

I'm going to present God's entrée to you as He prepared it, but here's a warning: the cut-off point for spiritual whiners was the last chapter! If you simply want to endure God's plan for your life and enjoy complaining about what God's doing to you, then you hit your watermark in the last chapter on perseverance.

Verse 3 tells us that we have everything we need for life—an amazingly abundant life capable of illuminating God's plan of reconciliation through the Holy Spirit—including grace given to us through the shed blood of Jesus Christ. In addition, we have everything we need for godliness. There's that word again—calling us to be like God. But again, what exactly does that mean?

Step 5: Godliness is a reverent loyalty to the obedient pursuit of Christlikeness.

In other words, we have everything we need to have a reverent loyalty to the obedient pursuit of Christlikeness. More specifically, we have everything we need to fulfill all the components of our passage in 2 Peter 1:4–8. In fact, in verse 3, we also see why godliness is a definition of the overall process of our passage, as well as one of the steps in that process.

In this introductory passage, Peter communicates a couple of assumptions in verse 3, which are necessary for our definition of godliness. First, Peter is assuming that you believe in a saving relationship with Jesus Christ. Second, you are committed to accepting the truth that God has given us everything we need to fulfill the transformation to Christlikeness. Those assumptions don't sound overwhelming by themselves. The power of these truths in verse 3 can be grasped as we break apart our definition of godliness and begin to understand what it takes to embrace all that God has allowed to affect us.

Godliness is a reverent loyalty to the obedient pursuit of Christlikeness.

The mystery word in our definition of godliness is *reverent*. It's a word with many misconceptions. It does not mean quiet, reserved, restrained, or stuffy. In fact, the dictionary definition talks about showing honor and devotion. It speaks of worship and adoration.

Basically, it means "to show honor and respect mixed with love and awe." These are words of passion, and they can help us understand what a reverent loyalty means. The word *reverent* means to be in awe of the character transformation we are undergoing, passionately excited about who we are becoming. To be godly, therefore, is not to simply endure God's will but to be deeply committed to the understanding that God is working everything we need for life and righteousness into our lives. This passage is not saying that we are to love the trials and tragedies of our lives, but that we are to trust in the greater goal of becoming Christlike for the glory of God.

Paul told the Thessalonians to "be joyful always and give thanks in all circumstances" (1 Thessalonians 5:16, 18 NIV). He challenged the Philippians to be content and driven by their trust in God over their circumstances (Philippians 1:12; 4:11). I am not going to tell you how you ought to feel as you walk through tragedy, trials, or times of silence because that is an individual faith response; although, I am going to say that we can come to a place where we accept that God is in control during these times. Godliness is about being loyal to the will of God through the good times and the bad.

So how can we add godliness to our faith? How do we add godliness and grasp that we have everything we need to have a reverent loyalty to the obedient pursuit of Christlikeness? How do we remain in awe of what God is doing *to* us so that we can be passionate about what He wants to do *through* us? I've found one of the greatest examples on how to answer that question in the life of Job.

The account of Job's life is one of the most difficult Scriptures to understand and embrace. His journey saw incredible lows and amazing highs all framed through his faith.

We're told,

> There was a man in the land of Uz whose name was Job; and that man was blameless, upright, fearing God and turning away from evil. Seven sons and

three daughters were born to him. His possessions also were 7,000 sheep, 3,000 camels, 500 yoke of oxen, 500 female donkeys, and very many servants; and that man was the greatest of all the men of the east.
—Job 1:1–3 (NASU)

Job had a great family and a ton of stuff. But his focus was on God, not people or possessions. How do we know?

Now there was a day when the sons of God came to present themselves before the Lord, and Satan also came among them. The Lord said to Satan, "From where do you come?" Then Satan answered the Lord and said, "From roaming about on the earth and walking around on it." The Lord said to Satan, "Have you considered My servant Job? For there is no one like him on the earth, a blameless and upright man, fearing God and turning away from evil."
—Job 1:6–8 (NASU)

Satan told God that the only reason Job loved Him was because he was blessed with many external things. Satan declared that if God removed Job's blessings, he would stray from his faith. So God gave permission for Job to be tested.

Now on the day when his sons and his daughters were eating and drinking wine in their oldest brother's house, a messenger came to Job and said, "The oxen were plowing and the donkeys feeding beside them, and the Sabeans attacked and took them. They also slew the servants with the edge of the sword, and I alone have escaped to tell you." While he was still speaking, another also came and said, "The fire of God fell from heaven and burned up the sheep and the servants and consumed them, and I alone have escaped to tell you." While he was still speaking, another also came and said, "The Chaldeans formed

three bands and made a raid on the camels and took them and slew the servants with the edge of the sword, and I alone have escaped to tell you." While he was still speaking, another also came and said, "Your sons and your daughters were eating and drinking wine in their oldest brother's house, and behold, a great wind came from across the wilderness and struck the four corners of the house, and it fell on the young people and they died, and I alone have escaped to tell you."
—Job 1:13–17 (NASU)

Every type of trial, test, or tragedy imaginable came upon Job. He lost everything, and at that point, Job had a few options for how he could respond to God. His wife gave him a strong suggestion in Job 2:9. "Then his wife said to him, 'Do you still hold fast your integrity? Curse God and die!'" His friends gave him other options in chapters 4–27. They told him to beg for mercy because these tragedies were God's punishment for his own sin.

So how did Job respond?

Then Job arose and tore his robe and shaved his head, and he fell to the ground and worshiped. He said, "Naked I came from my mother's womb, and naked I shall return there. The LORD gave and the LORD has taken away. Blessed be the name of the LORD." Through all this Job did not sin nor did he blame God.
—Job 1:20–22 (NASU)

Job really was "the greatest man among all the people of the East" (Job 1:3 NIV)! Job understood that his greatest blessing was not the existence of *external* things but the *internal* presence of God. The presence of God, though, does not mean the absence of trials. Paul acknowledged that when he said, "We are hard pressed on every side, but not crushed; perplexed, but not in despair; persecuted, but not abandoned; struck down, but not destroyed" (2 Corinthians 4:9 NIV). Job was broken as he walked through these dark days. In fact, as he faced these tragedies, his health was taken from him. Just as anyone would, he went through grief, desperation, and questioning God.

> Afterward Job opened his mouth and cursed the day of his birth. And Job said, "Let the day perish on which I was to be born, and the night which said, 'A boy is conceived.' May that day be darkness; Let not God above care for it, nor light shine on it. Let darkness and black gloom claim it; Let a cloud settle on it; Let the blackness of the day terrify it. As for that night, let darkness seize it; Let it not rejoice among the days of the year; Let it not come into the number of the months. Behold, let that night be barren; Let no joyful shout enter it. Let those curse it who curse the day, who are prepared to rouse Leviathan. Let the stars of its twilight be darkened; Let it wait for light but have none, And let it not see the breaking dawn; Because it did not shut the opening of my mother's womb, Or hide trouble from my eyes. Why did I not die at birth, Come forth from the womb and expire?
> —Job 3:1–11 (NASU)

Job hated what he was going through. Job 29:1 says that he longed to go back to life before all of this started. But he refused to give up on God. Do you remember Job's wife and her advice to him? "Curse God and die," she said. His response back to her is one of the greatest verses in all of Scripture when it comes to spiritual transformation. He said to her, "You speak as one of the foolish women speaks. Shall we indeed accept good from God and not accept adversity?" In all this, Job did not sin with his lips (Job 2:10 NASU). With that statement, Job revealed his godliness, his reverent loyalty to the obedient pursuit of becoming like God.

Job was not perfect, and God wanted to show him some things in his own spiritual journey through these dark days. In fact, in Job 29–31, he begins to waiver. He begins to question God about why this had to happen to him. Job had been saying all the right things, but his friends had started to get to him. He begins to justify to himself that God should not have done these things to him. Job started listening to voices around him. His friends were encouraging him to use the tragedies in his life as a license to sin. They told him God had let him down, and they urged him to give up on God.

Personally, I've walked through some dark days, too. Most of us have at some point in our lives. Years ago, I was forced to walk through something that was crushing me. Those were probably the darkest days of my life. The stress was affecting my work, my home, and my marriage. I was angry, and I questioned God. I found myself not looking for God's direction but struggling through anger as my flesh began to justify my desire to sin. Thankfully, God brought me to a place in His Word and spoke to me through the same answer He gave to Job.

> Then the LORD answered Job out of the storm. He said: "Who is this that darkens my counsel with words without knowledge? Brace yourself like a man; I will question you, and you shall answer me. Where were you when I laid the earth's foundation? Tell me, if you understand. Who marked off its dimensions? Surely you know! Who stretched a measuring line across it?"
> —Job 38:1–5 (NIV)

Job complained to God that he was suffering needlessly. Many people might think that God should have responded by cutting Job a break. Job was in the same place I was. He didn't need to see God's sorrow. Instead, he needed to recognize God's strength. *When we go through tough times, we don't want to simply know of God's presence; we want to be assured of His power.* As thoughts of sin and doubt crept into the mind of Job, God responded with strength and assured Job that not only was He present, but He was in control. God's response brought Job back to God's presence and to his knees.

Then Job replied to the LORD: "I know that you can do all things; no plan of yours can be thwarted. You asked, 'Who is this that obscures my counsel without knowledge?' Surely I spoke of things I did not understand, things too wonderful for me to know. You said, 'Listen now, and I will speak; I will question you, and you shall answer me.' My ears had heard of you but now my eyes have seen you. Therefore I despise myself and repent in dust and ashes."
—Job 42:1–6 (NIV)

Job confessed and renewed his commitment to a life of godliness—a reverent loyalty to the obedient pursuit of Christlikeness. God was no longer a distant religious idea but a living necessity in his life. "My ears had heard of you but now my eyes have seen you" (Job 42:5 NIV). Job finally experienced God beyond a mere knowledge of Him. Job's story reminds us that we can live faithfully and still face the tragedies of a world fallen in sin.

When we go through tough times, we don't want to simply know of God's presence; we want to be assured of His power.

Faithfulness is not the guarantee some may claim to a life without issues. In fact, we see throughout the New Testament that faithfulness brings persecution. I would challenge you to check yourself. If you're not feeling some sense of persecution due to your faith, look to your right and left. You might be running with the devil instead of against him. The apostle Paul prayed passionately for those who were faithfully living out their faith. "For this reason also, since the day we heard this, we haven't stopped praying for you" (Colossians 1:9 HCSB). "For this reason" refers to a report sent to Paul from Epaphras, (the man who was more than likely the church planter for the church in Colossae). And you would think, based on Paul's response, that he must have received a bad report about the spiritual health of the church. If you came into the conversation and heard Paul say that he would not stop praying for them, you might think, *Boy, there must be trouble,* but in reality, Epaphras gave Paul an encouraging report about the church. As we see in verse 9, it's the positive report that caused Paul to increase his resolve to pray for them.

Now I know it may seem unnecessary and even counterculture to pray for those who are doing well. Much of our prayer time focuses on those who are struggling in life, facing difficulties, fallen into sin, or dealing with a physical issue; however, Paul knew that the church's spiritual growth and their devotion to godliness did not give him permission to stop praying for them. Instead, it deepened his resolve to pray for their continued growth and protection.

Paul had seen firsthand how the enemy reserves his strongest opposition for those who have the most potential for expanding God's glory. So instead of celebrating and moving on to the next prayer request, Paul had a specific prayer for this church: "We are asking that you may be filled with the knowledge of His will in all wisdom and spiritual understanding" (Colossians 1:9b HCSB). Paul prayed that the Colossians "be filled with the knowledge of His will." The word *filled* used here means to be completely filled or filled to the top. A more practical picture of the word *filled* being used in this passage is to be totally controlled. It's the same word describing the disciples who were filled with the Holy Spirit (Acts 4:31) as well as Stephen, who was full of faith (Acts 6:5). They were totally under the control of what *filled* them.

Paul wanted the Colossians to be totally controlled by *knowledge (epignœsis,* eh-pig-a-no-sis). Paul picked this word to clearly communicate his desire for the Colossians to have a deep and thorough knowledge of what God wanted from them. The word he used communicates his desire for them to be great learners— to get it! "I pray that your participation in the faith may become effective through **knowing** every good thing that is in us for the glory of Christ" (Philemon 6 NIV). Paul prayed for the effectiveness of Philemon's faith through the knowledge (same Greek word: epignœsis) of what we have in us through Christ. We've already stated that godliness is not an issue of information but an issue of obedience—"so that you may walk worthy of the Lord" (Colossians 1:10 HCSB).

With the phrase to *walk worthy,* Paul is referring to our daily journey. The *walk* is our daily spiritual journey determined by the steps of our decisions, and those decisions lead to our actions. The word *worthy* used here comes from a root word meaning "to balance the scales." You work a day's labor, you earn a day's wage. Paul is telling the readers that here, in Christ, you have already received your reward. Your pay was given before you did a thing. Christ calls us into salvation and paid the debt of sin in full, giving those of us in Christ the positions of sons and daughters. Already having received our payment, our scale is heavy with the payments of blessing. To *walk worthy* is to balance the scale, to walk as one who has been given the high position as a child of God and fellow heir with Jesus Christ and now wants to balance the scale. He's saying that we should live a life that matches our spiritual position. A life totally controlled by God's Word, His wisdom, and understanding produces a life worthy of the Lord, a life of godliness.

Living for Christ is extremely difficult when we feel the need to make the decisions. It's much easier when we trust the Holy Spirit. We tell God, "Well, I think," and the Holy Spirit says, "Umm, no! Do what I said to do." It's a decision of obedience. When we do obey, we are *fully pleasing to Him.* Our spiritual goal can never be to partially please God!

> Yes, Lord, walking in the way of your laws, we wait for you; your name and renown are the desire of our hearts. My soul yearns for you in the night; in the morning my spirit longs for you. When your judgments come upon the earth, the people of the world learn righteousness.
> —Isaiah 26:8–9 (NIV)

How do we know if our lives are fully pleasing to Him? We will be *bearing fruit in every good work.*

Fruit is the by-product of godliness. Fruit refers to multiple things in the New Testament, including character transformation through the fruits of the Spirit (Galatians 5:22–23), winning others to the Lord (1 Corinthians 16:15), and worship and praise (Hebrews 13:15). Spiritual fruit is the outward evidence of an inward transformation. To bear *fruit in every good work* is a lifetime journey. Peter lays out the path of this journey in our focal passage:

> For this very reason, make every effort to supplement your faith with goodness, goodness with knowledge, knowledge with self-control, self-control with endurance, endurance with godliness, godliness with brotherly affection, and brotherly affection with love. For if these qualities are yours and are increasing, they will keep you from being useless or unfruitful in the knowledge of our Lord Jesus Christ.
> —2 Peter 1:5–8 (HCSB)

Look at verse 8. "They will keep you from being useless or unfruitful in the knowledge of our Lord Jesus Christ." What a description! *Useless or unfruitful in the knowledge.* This is Paul's prayer for the church in Colossae, that they'll be *growing in the knowledge of God.*

Here's that word *knowledge* again. Paul is praying something crazy, that by being totally controlled by the knowledge of God, they will be growing in the knowledge of God. How does that work? Scripture says it's a mystery. "We speak God's hidden wisdom in a mystery, which God predestined before the ages for our glory" (1 Corinthians 2:7 HCSB). God is a mystery to those outside of His Word! The more we trust God's Word, however, the more we're controlled by God's Word. The more we're controlled by God's Word, the more we'll love God's Word. The more we love God's Word, the more we'll reflect God's Word, and that's godliness.

Study Questions

Intro video for group study can be found at
www.myjourneydeeper.com

1. Discuss the author's definition for the characteristic of godliness: godliness is a reverent loyalty to the obedient pursuit of Christlikeness.

2. Why do you think God made godliness a step in the journey to godliness (Christlikeness)?

3. How do you connect to Job's journey?

4. What is the difference between simply knowing God is present and knowing that God is in control?

5. What happens when you try to partially please God?

6. What did you learn from this chapter, and how can you apply it to your life?

7. What areas do you need to pray about or improve in your walk with Jesus?

Chapter 7
A Whole New Level

Step 1: Moral excellence is the God-given ability to perform heroic deeds.

Step 2: Knowledge is the truth of God properly comprehended and applied.

Step 3: Self-control is the restraint to trust the will of God over the will of self.

Step 4: Perseverance is the spiritual staying power that gives believers the courage to literally die instead of rejecting the faith.

Step 5: Godliness is a reverent loyalty to the obedient pursuit of Christlikeness.

add to your faith
Brotherly Kindness

Early in my diving experiences, I was told that one day we would be diving deep enough to experience thermocline—the point in the water where the heat of the sun can't reach and where we would experience a dramatic shift in the temperature of the water. I was thoroughly intrigued with the idea of being where the effects of the sun couldn't reach, but I was curious if it would be a gradual change that I might barely feel or a dramatic change at a certain level. One morning, Dr. Mignerey made sure we all brought full wet suits, which we thought might be a little overkill for the gulf waters in late summer. He promised, though, that they would be necessary.

As I dove into the water, I was excited about what I would experience, but I was trying to control my breathing and not use too much of my air on the way down. Watching my gauges, I knew I was getting close to the depth mark for the thermocline. Still feeling the warmth from the sun's effects on the water, I was thinking that perhaps I didn't really need the wet suit and that maybe the wet suit might be preventing me from knowing when I passed the thermocline mark. Yet, as we continued to descend, I kept a heightened awareness of my temperature, hoping to experience any change at all.

Suddenly, with one more stroke of my fins, I almost swallowed my regulator due to the severe change in the water temperature. Dr. Mignerey was not kidding! It was a clear line, and I knew exactly when I crossed it. In addition, I could no longer distinguish color, and the darkness was amazingly pure. There was no doubt that I had crossed a line and had entered a whole new deeper level in my adventure.

Much like an unexpected temperature change as you head into deeper waters, our next characteristic in the pursuit of a Christ-like image for our lives is unexpected. It may seem out of order in this journey or even easy to overlook. As we will see in the pages ahead, it will truly mark a whole new level of faith. In Philippians 3:14 (NASU), Paul said, "I press on toward the goal for the prize of the upward call of God in Christ Jesus." What goal? The goal of becoming conformed to the image of Christ. What prize? To be standing in the overwhelming presence of God and His glory. There is no greater prize, no more perfect place than the presence of God. The closer we get to the core of Christ's character, you will see, the more that image will differ with the images of the world.

Our next characteristic in our journey is brotherly kindness. In the next few pages, we will unpack why kindness is a much deeper and more important step than it may seem in this process to becoming more like Christ. First, I know it is completely a God thing for the word *brotherly* to be in front of *kindness* because the world has labeled kindness as a mostly feminine emotion. Men are rough, and women are kind, right? Men and women do have significantly different characteristics, but Scripture tells us kindness is a character quality of Christlikeness having nothing to do with gender. We need to stop seeing kindness as a weakness and start seeing it as a core characteristic of Christ. I want us to look at a better biblical definition of what it means to add brotherly kindness to our faith.

Step 6: Brotherly kindness is the selflessness to be a living sacrifice.

The best scriptural definition of brotherly kindness is Philippians 2:3–8 (NASU).

> Do nothing from selfishness or empty conceit, but with humility of mind regard one another as more important than yourselves; do not merely look out for your own personal interests, but also for the interests of others. Have this attitude in yourselves which was also in Christ Jesus, who, although He existed in the form of God, did not regard equality with God a thing to be grasped, but emptied Himself, taking the form of a bondservant, and being made in the likeness of men. Being found in appearance as a man, He humbled Himself by becoming obedient to the point of death, even death on a cross.

When we begin to ask ourselves what it means to walk in the selflessness of being a living sacrifice, we have to begin with Philippians 2:6. Christ is God with every right, privilege, and authority that comes with being God; however, Jesus laid aside his divine rights for the Father's will. In fact, He could not even grasp the concept of selfishness. For sinful man to become reconciled before a Holy God, Jesus was willing to be a living sacrifice.

Brotherly kindness is the selflessness to be a living sacrifice.

Let's step back and talk about rights for a second. Rights are birthed out of a perceived entitlement. The common thought is that, "I deserve something, so I'm going to do whatever it takes to take full advantage of my rights." Have you ever wondered why the apostles of the New Testament began each letter describing themselves as servants of Jesus Christ and not as friends of Jesus? Stop and look at the first verse of books written by Paul, Peter, and James. The Greek word *doulos* keeps reappearing, which is interpreted as "bond servant" or "slave." Jesus had called them His friends in John 15:15, so why not use that impressive title? Why continually refer to yourself as a slave?

I love the answer to that question from the book of Deuteronomy:

> If your fellow Hebrew, a man or woman, is sold to you and serves you six years, you must set him free in the seventh year. When you set him free, do not send him away empty-handed. Give generously to him from your flock, your threshing floor, and your winepress. You are to give him whatever the Lord your God has blessed you with. Remember that you were a slave in the land of Egypt and the Lord your God redeemed you; that is why I am giving you this command today. But if your slave says to you, "I don't want to leave you," because he loves you and your family, and is well off with you, take an awl and pierce through his ear into the door, and he will become your slave for life. Also treat your female slave the same way.
> —Deuteronomy 15:12–18 (HCSB)

In ancient Israel, when a Hebrew man or woman could not care for themselves, they could sell themselves into slavery. These were people who could not make it on their own, so they turned to a master who could provide for them. They would work out a six-year commitment, and in the seventh year, the master would set them free. Furthermore, the passage tells us that the master was not supposed to send the newly freed slave back out into the world empty-handed. Instead, he should send him into his freedom with everything he or she needed for their new life. *Give generously to him from your flock.* Flocks determined wealth and gave the freed slave a new source of income. *Your threshing floor, and your winepress.* Grain and wine would give them food and drink to get started in their new life. The master generously gave the newly freed slave everything needed to start an abundant new life. Sound familiar? These are the words Jesus spoke to us, "I have come that they may have life and have it in abundance" (John 10:10b HCSB).

This picture of a slave and his master is also a picture of our own salvation. In our own sin, we have become separated from a holy God and cannot come back to God on our own. We cannot do it ourselves! Our master Jesus Christ, however, has taken us in and provided a home for us. When a master gave his slave freedom, he would send the freed slave out the door with an abundance of food, drink, and the resources needed to work and start a new abundant life. This is an image of the very life given to Christ followers when they come into a new life with Jesus Christ. We get freedom, but we also get so much more—an abundant life with everything we need in our freedom to have an amazing new life.

The picture of Paul, Peter, James, and any of Christ's followers who have died to self is the image of verse 16. The slave asks the master, "Where could I go in my freedom that is better than being here with you? I give my new life back to you, and in my freedom, I bow down and honor you! I am going to stay with you! I came to you out of need, and I am going to stay out of love" (my paraphrase). Now, in one of those crazy Old Testament moments, we see the master take the slave and nail him to the master's front door by means of an awl through the slave's ear. Couldn't the master just have said, "Thank you"? I'm afraid there was no celebration, just a hole in the ear to serve as a visual statement that this slave chose to stay with his master.

Today, when we choose Christ, we do not get a nail through the ear. We get a filling of the Holy Spirit allowing us to also bear the marks of our master's house. Everyone knew the slave's heart by the fact that he carried the mark of his master's house. When we allow the Holy Spirit to transform us into the image of Christ, we are bearing the marks of our master's house! Character transformation is the mark of our Master's house. You see, kindness is one of those characteristics people try to downplay by saying, "It's not in my personality" or "It doesn't fit who I am." But that doesn't matter. As God's slave, I now bear the marks of my master's house. I'm dead to my own desires and choose to only display the character of my master. But what about my spiritual rights, my Christian liberties? Scripture tells us that we have been crucified with Christ. We surrendered our lives to Him so that as "we died with Christ, we believe we will also live with him" (Romans 6:8 HCSB). We must remember: dead men have no rights. When you were made alive in Christ, you gained a whole new world full of freedoms, and ultimately, you nailed your rights to the same cross where Jesus nailed your sins.

Character transformation is the mark of our Master's house.

I'll have to admit that kindness does not come naturally to me. It flies in direct opposition to my flesh. I'm an American, which means I know all about my rights and how to crush you if you interfere with those rights. As a Christ follower, though, I'm called to lay aside my rights and commit to Matthew 16:24–25 (NIV), which says, "If anyone would come after me, he must deny himself and take up his cross and follow me. For whoever wants to save his life will lose it, but whoever loses his life for me will find it." So the only way I'm going to learn how to add brotherly kindness to my pursuit of the image of Christ is to understand what it means to be a living sacrifice. Paul tells the Romans to offer their bodies as a living sacrifice.

> Therefore, brothers, by the mercies of God, I urge you to present your bodies as a living sacrifice, holy and pleasing to God; this is your spiritual worship. Do not be conformed to this age, but be transformed by the renewing of your mind, so that you may discern what is the good, pleasing, and perfect will of God.
> —Romans 12:1–2 (HCSB)

I'll give you an example of someone selfless enough to be a true living sacrifice. In the book of Genesis, God tells Abraham to show his devotion to God by offering up his teenage son, Isaac, as a sacrifice. Abraham was confused and broken, but he obeyed God. When Abraham, who was pushing one hundred years old, told his teenage son to lie on the altar, Isaac allowed himself to be bound and be completely vulnerable to the will of his father.

> Then they came to the place of which God had told him; and Abraham built the altar there and arranged the wood, and bound his son Isaac and laid him on the altar, on top of the wood.
> —Genesis 22:9 (NASU)

Isaac could have refused and walked away, but he accepted the will of his father and became a living sacrifice. Here's the lesson in Isaac's willingness to be sacrificed: brotherly kindness is transformed into the lives of those willing to lie vulnerable on God's altar. As believers, we need to stop squirming around on God's altar and allow Him the authority to use us as His arms and feet in a world where the characteristic of kindness is dying. Today, selfishness is no longer a sin but the guiding standard of our society. We need to reach the point where relationships are dearer to us than our rights. We live in a world that is desperate to see the kindness of Christ, and I want to spend the rest of our time in this chapter looking at one of my favorite stories in all of Scripture and one amazing Old Testament model for brotherly kindness.

Let me give you a little background on the story of Jonathan and his kindness to David. Saul was the first king of Israel, and his son, Jonathan, was the heir apparent to the throne. Jonathan had every skill needed to be a great king for Israel. He was loved by the people; they were willing to die for him. He was a great warrior and leader, had a sharp mind, and most importantly, he loved God and followed His commands. There is no doubt that he would be considered one the greatest kings in that nation's history. But there was one problem. He never became king. God told Jonathan that it was His will for David, Jonathan's best friend, to be king. Jonathan had a couple of choices about how to handle this news and about how he'd treat David.

> Now it came about when he had finished speaking to Saul, that the soul of Jonathan was knit to the soul of David, and Jonathan loved him as himself. Saul took him that day and did not let him return to his father's house. Then Jonathan made a **covenant** with David because he loved him as himself. Jonathan stripped himself of the robe that was on him and gave it to David, with his armor, including his sword and his bow and his belt.
> —1 Samuel 18:1–4 (NASU)

Jonathan could have hated David and resented God for giving his position to someone else, but he didn't. He loved David and went out of his way to help David succeed. In fact, Scripture says Jonathan made a covenant with David. Remember in a previous chapter we discussed that a covenant is a transformational relationship. Jonathan was willing to transform who he was to fulfill who God wanted David to be. Jonathan was no less important to God than David. He simply had different plans for their lives, plans that each brought glory to God. Here's a truth we all need to learn: demonstrating obedient kindness does not lessen God's plan for your life but allows you to be used by God to fulfill His plan in someone else's life.

Remember what Philippians 2:3–4 (NASU) tells us about brotherly kindness.

> Do nothing from selfishness or empty conceit, but with humility of mind regard one another as more important than yourselves; do not merely look out for your own personal interests, but also for the interests of others.

Jonathan did what it took for God's will to be obeyed in both of their lives; however, Jonathan took it even farther. Jonathan actually equipped David to succeed by stripping off his robe and giving it to David, along with his sword, bow, and belt. Jonathan was not only willing to transform who he was to fulfill who God wanted David to be, but he was also willing to surrender back to God the resources God had given him. Brotherly kindness will call you to give back from the resources God has given you. Time, finances, possessions, comfort—at some level, kindness costs!

Jonathan was willing to pay the price of obedient kindness to his brother because, in the end, Jonathan was less concerned about his own legacy and more concerned about the purposes of God. Please understand that when you have gone this far into the character of Christ, you need to know brotherly kindness is much deeper than mere courtesies. The characteristic of brotherly kindness that conforms us to the image of Christ moves us away from our own legacy and allows us to connect with the legacy of God.

Brotherly kindness is the selflessness to be a living sacrifice. "Be kind to one another, tenderhearted, forgiving each other, just as God in Christ also has forgiven you" (Ephesians 4:32 NASU).

Study Questions

Intro video for group study can be found at
www.myjourneydeeper.com

1. Discuss the author's definition for the characteristic of brotherly kindness: brotherly kindness is the selflessness to be a living sacrifice.

2. Does kindness seem out of place this deep in the journey to Christlikeness?

3. What can we learn from the disciples and apostles who called themselves *doulos* (slaves)?

4. What marks from our Master's house should we carry?

5. What do we learn in this chapter about the character of Jonathan?

6. What did you learn from this chapter, and how can you apply it to your life?

7. What areas do you need to pray about or improve in your walk with Jesus?

Chapter 8
Deeper Than You Think

Step 1: Moral excellence is the God-given ability to perform heroic deeds.

Step 2: Knowledge is the truth of God properly comprehended and applied.

Step 3: Self-control is the restraint to trust the will of God over the will of self.

Step 4: Perseverance is the spiritual staying power that gives believers the courage to literally die instead of rejecting the faith.

Step 5: Godliness is a reverent loyalty to the obedient pursuit of Christlikeness.

Step 6: Brotherly Kindness is the selflessness of being a living sacrifice.

add to your faith
Love

Lori and I decided to give each other a cruise to the Bahamas for our first anniversary. We had to save our Christmas money, birthday money, loose change, and anything we could set aside to do it, but it was so worth it. Lori found out that one of the excursions was an afternoon of diving off the coast of the Bahamas in the crystal-clear waters of the Caribbean, so she made sure I got signed up for the day. I couldn't wait.

When the day arrived, we loaded up our equipment and went out to a spot with a sunken ship on one side and an amazing coral reef on the other. I remember so clearly being shocked to see the bottom and worried that we were diving in water that was too shallow. I was worried until the guide on the dive explained that we were staring fifty feet down and that what we saw was deeper than what we thought.

I've never forgotten the problem with depth perception I had that day. I could not have guessed the depth of the water and the adventure that awaited me on that dive—a day filled with bright living coral formations, sunken ships, and sharks. I loved it but never saw it coming.

Sometimes, our spiritual depth perception can be way off. But thankfully God has prepared us for the depth of the characteristic in front of us as we have finally reached the heart of spiritual transformation. Where God takes us in this chapter will be something that you'll never see coming. The transformation from my flesh, my ways, my desires into the image of Christ ends with the most difficult characteristic known to man: love. It's the characteristic that draws us most to the very image of Christ. Love is built on all the other characteristics we've explored in our focal passage, and it is the one Christ spent the most time defending to the church.

> You have heard that it was said, "YOU SHALL LOVE YOUR NEIGHBOR and hate your enemy." But I say to you, love your enemies and pray for those who persecute you, so that you may be sons of your Father who is in heaven; for He causes His sun to rise on the evil and the good, and sends rain on the righteous and the unrighteous. For if you love those who love you, what reward do you have? Do not even the tax collectors do the same? If you greet only your brothers, what more

are you doing than others? Do not even the Gentiles
do the same? Therefore you are to be perfect, as your
heavenly Father is perfect.
Matthew 5:43–48 (NASU)

Where did that word *perfect* come from? Let's examine it in
context. Jesus is talking about loving your enemies, a concept that
was uncommon for that culture. He developed the concept more
in verses 46 and 47 when he talked about the pursuit of the world
to simply "love their own," but for those pursuing the glory of God,
Jesus calls us to something greater: perfection. In this passage, Jesus
is speaking about a perfection that can only be reached through
love. So how will we define love?

Step 7: Love is the surrendered choice of dying to self so others can experience Christ.

The love mentioned in our focal passage is not a puppy-dog love
between young people. It's not the *phileo* love between brothers or
friends. It's not even the passion you feel for your spouse. It is *agape*
love, which was best demonstrated on the cross and is best achieved
by man in the two commandments Jesus listed as the greatest.

> One of the scribes approached. When he heard them
> debating and saw that Jesus answered them well,
> he asked Him, "Which commandment is the most
> important of all?" "This is the most important," Jesus
> answered: "Listen, Israel! The Lord our God, The Lord
> is One. Love the Lord your God with all your heart,
> with all your soul, with all your mind, and with all
> your strength. The second is: Love your neighbor as
> yourself. There is no other commandment greater
> than these."
> —Mark 12:28–31 (HCSB)

At the time this conversation took place, Jesus had already made

His triumphal entry into Jerusalem. He had cursed the fig tree for not producing fruit. He had cleared the temple of those who would steal God's offerings for worthless sacrifices. He had had His authority questioned, and on Tuesday of His last week, He was preaching in the temple. It had been a day of intense debate, a war of wits and words with the Sadducees, Pharisees, and Herodians. They had been trying to trap Jesus, asking Him what would appear to be honest, straightforward questions. But most of the questions would have been a no-win situation for anyone other than Jesus. Looking at the hearts of the men questioning Jesus, it really wasn't much of a contest.

Love is the surrendered choice of dying to self so others can experience Christ.

As with any debate, this one had attracted a sizeable crowd, including a scribe. He listened and loved it when the Sadducees tried to stump Jesus with a question about the resurrection. The scribe might have gotten caught up in the moment and really wanted answers, or maybe he thought his question could stump Jesus. Either way, it is a great question for us too. What is the greatest commandment? What is the priority of God? Above all else, what does God want us to do? To unconditionally love God with all of our heart, mind, soul, and strength and to love others as we love ourselves. In these words, we find our definition for love and see the very heart of Christlikeness.

Agape love is an unconditional pursuit of God, which produces an unconditional compassion for man. Before that blows your mind, let me assure you that you will not be able to muster *agape* love on your own, even if you spend a lifetime trying. *Agape* love is given to each believer in our new nature. When we give our lives to Christ and God moves us from "dead in our trespasses" to "alive in His grace," that new nature carries with it the capacity to love. The apostle John put it bluntly:

> Beloved, let us love one another, for love is from God;
> and everyone who loves is born of God and knows
> God. The one who does not love does not know
> God, for God is love. By this the love of God was
> manifested in us, that God has sent His only begotten
> Son into the world so that we might live through Him.
> —1 John 4:7–9 (NASU)

Agape love is a God-given characteristic; however, having a particular quality and using it effectively are two different things. Our focal passage in 2 Peter tells us effective love is built on all the characteristics we've discussed in previous chapters. That's why Peter told us to add to our faith moral excellence and to add to our moral excellence, knowledge, etc. *Agape* love is the choice to surrender the desire of self—to die to self—so you can unconditionally pursue God and allow Him to show you others through His eyes.

How do you die to self? You remove the burden of decision making off your shoulders and replace it with obedience to God. Following is the easiest position in life. Leading is the most difficult, and wanting to lead from a follower's position is the most frustrating. When we die to ourselves, we are accepting God's plan for our lives even when God's will takes us in a direction contrary to our own will. Elizabeth Elliot, in her program *Gateway to Joy*, stated it this way: "The cross means the will of God crosses the will of man and somebody has to die." Why? The easiest answer I can give you is that the nature of man can only love in circumstances pleasing to self, while the nature of God (the Spirit) can and does love unconditionally. When we die to ourselves and replace our desires with the will of God, we gain the capacity to love unconditionally. That's when we begin the daily battle to surrender self to the Spirit.

Think about it this way: What or whom do you love? And why?

- I love ice cream and candy because they bring me pleasure.

- I love golf because it brings me satisfaction.

- I love my calling or job because it brings me significance.

- I love my children because they bring me delight and meaning.

- I love my wife because I delight in her beauty, I feel secure in her embrace, and I find joy in her words.

We invest in those things we love, and we love those things that bring us pleasure, satisfaction, significance, delight, and security. We think the things we love provide these emotions for us, but from God's point of view, these things are nothing compared to Him. The things we long for the most are all found in Him.

> You reveal the path of life to me; in Your presence is abundant joy; in Your right hand are eternal pleasures.
> —Psalm 16:11 (HCSB)

> Take delight in the Lord, and He will give you your heart's desires.
> —Psalm 37:4 (HCSB)

So if it is the priority of God for us to love God and love others, what does it mean exactly to love God? When we talk about loving God with all our heart, mind, soul, and strength, we are saying that loving God means focusing all our longings on Him. Why would we ever not love God with all our heart, mind, soul, and strength? John Piper, in his book *A Hunger for God,* summed up our problem by stating, "The weakness of our hunger for God is not because He is unsavory, but because we keep ourselves stuffed with other things."

How do I take all the things I love, put them in their proper place, and discover the joy of God's love? Here's the key: *I must recognize that in Him—not from Him—is the true joy of love and life.* Man's purpose is not to pursue the blessings of God but to pursue the loving presence of God. The beauty of heaven is not the trappings of the place but the knowledge that in heaven, we find the full presence of God. He is the goal of heaven!

To love the Lord your God with all your heart, soul, mind, and strength is a call to action.

To love God with all our heart is to passionately pursue God's presence.

To love God with all our soul is to be spiritually hungry, even desperate, for the eternity that He alone has secured for us.

To love God with all our mind is to be satisfied in the wisdom that allows us to intimately know Him.

To love God with all our strength is to physically surrender our lives to His incredible will.

God gave us the greatest commandment, but He added a second commandment that says, "The second is: Love your neighbor as yourself" (Mark 12:31a, HCSB).

To love your neighbor is the visible manifestation of loving God.

Jesus couldn't give only the first commandment. In other words, you can't love God with everything you are without it resulting in loving your neighbor. How then do we love others? We love them and treat them as we want to be loved, as we want to be treated.

> For no one ever hates his own flesh, but provides and
> cares for it, just as Christ does for the church.
> —Ephesians 5:29 (HCSB)

> Therefore, whatever you want others to do for you,
> do also the same for them—this is the Law and the
> Prophets.
> —Matthew 7:12 (HCSB)

It may have been toward the end of His ministry before Jesus clearly stated what the greatest commandments were, but He had already spent three years teaching them. And it seems like every time Jesus taught about loving others, somebody wanted clarification. Love my neighbor, but who's my neighbor? Forgive others, but exactly how often do I need to forgive others? We might not like it, nor want to do it, but the greatest act of love we can show to others is the same act of love someone showed to us: forgiveness. Whatever we seek, we will find in God; whatever we find in God, we must offer to others. Look at this story from the life of Jesus:

> So many people gathered together that there was no more room, not even in the doorway, and He was speaking the message to them. Then they came to Him bringing a paralytic, carried by four men. Since they were not able to bring him to Jesus because of the crowd, they removed the roof above where He was. And when they had broken through, they lowered the stretcher on which the paralytic was lying. Seeing their faith, Jesus told the paralytic, "Son, your sins are forgiven."
> —Mark 2:2–5 (HCSB)

I love this story! What a beautiful picture of *faith*: four friends' commitment to bring their paralytic friend to Jesus. All of my life, I've celebrated this account for the physical healing of the man brought to Jesus by the faith of his friends. But lately, as I've looked at this passage, I want to show you something about this encounter that is different from some of the *other* healings mentioned in Scripture. What is one thing consistent with these other miracles that is not present with this man or his friends?

> Then a man with a serious skin disease came to Him and, on his knees, begged Him: "If You are willing, You can make me clean."
> —Mark 1:40 (HCSB)

> Now the woman was Greek, a Syrophoenician by birth, and she kept asking Him to drive the demon out of her daughter.
> —Mark 7:26 (HCSB)

> Out of the crowd, one man answered Him, "Teacher, I brought my son to You. He has a spirit that makes him unable to speak."
> —Mark 9:17 (HCSB)

> Then Jesus answered him, "What do you want Me to do for you?" "Rabbouni," the blind man told Him, "I want to see!"
> —Mark 10:51 (HCSB)

In all these accounts, someone is asking to be physically healed. Someone is basically saying, "Jesus, something is physically wrong, and I want you to fix it." When we come back to the account in Mark 2, these men brought their friend to Jesus and *verbally* asked for nothing. The friends didn't shout down to Jesus, "Heal our friend!" The man didn't look up at Jesus and beg to be healed. *In a moment of silence*, Jesus saw the faith of the friends and then turned to the man and dealt with his greatest need. "Son, your sins are forgiven." What an odd thing to say to a man with an obvious physical disability! In the days of Jesus, however, physical disabilities were *seen as* a sign of God's disapproval, as a sign of sin. Even the disciples bought into this belief, and in a different encounter with a blind man, they questioned Jesus about it.

> As He was passing by, He saw a man blind from birth. His disciples questioned Him: "Rabbi, who sinned, this man or his parents, that he was born blind?"
> —John 9:1–2 (HCSB)

Disabilities are not a sign of God's disapproval. They are a natural result of living in a world filled with disease and death.

Now, we assume the man lying in front of Jesus wanted to walk. Yet it wasn't the determination of the friends that moved Jesus; it was their *faith*. In a culture constantly condemning the paralytic man for his sins, could his friends have successfully convinced him of how important he was to God, how valuable he was to God, how much God loved him? Would they be outmatched by *the resounding accusations of sin* by the community around them?

His whole life, he had been told his disability was a sign of God's disappointment with him. He was imprisoned on a mat, forced to listen to the condemnation of others, constantly feeling worthless, and struggling through constant guilt. Every day, he was found lying on his mat, staring at the ceiling, unable to do anything but try to figure out what he had done to make God so upset with him. "Why would God leave me imprisoned in this body?"

Then God allowed me to see another side to this story. Could it be that I focus so much on the physical healing because I approach the power of forgiveness with such little regard? I've always focused on the physical healing. I had only thought, "Praise God, Jesus physically healed him!" It never even crossed my mind that there was something deeper that needed to be healed. What if these men were incredible saints of faith? Faithful saints in an unfaithful time. What if what they came to do was done before he was ever physically healed? Could that have been the end of the encounter if the religious leaders hadn't begun to think to themselves?

> But some of the scribes were sitting there, thinking to themselves: "Why does He speak like this? He's blaspheming! Who can forgive sins but God alone?"
> —Mark 2:6–7 (HCSB)

His healing was the physical confirmation of the divine power of God standing right in front of them. Now, more than likely, physical healing was at least part of the original desire of these men. I'm sure they hoped it would be a part of the encounter. But Jesus stayed true to His message that the spiritual is the priority. Repentance was of greater importance than walking. Jesus' love for this man went so much deeper than his physical need. These friends risked a lot to show their friend how much God loved him. Jesus demonstrated his love first through the meeting of this man's greatest need: God's forgiveness.

Jesus ultimately showed this man, and all of us, His love for us when He died for our sins. The greatest act of love in the entire world was God's sacrifice for our sins. Forgiveness and love don't sound like the deepest thing you can know or do in your spiritual journey; however, there is nothing deeper than forgiveness and love when shown to others the way God has poured them on you.

Love is the surrendered choice of dying to self so others can experience Christ.

Study Questions

Intro video for group study can be found at
www.myjourneydeeper.com

1. Discuss the author's definition for the characteristic of love: love is the surrendered choice of dying to self so others can experience Christ.

2. How do we love God with all our heart? (What does that look like practically?)

   • How do we love God with all our mind? (What does that look like practically?)

   • How do we love God with all our soul? (What does that look like practically?)

   • How do we love God with all our strength? (What does that look like practically?)

3. How does our love for God affect our love for others?

4. How are love and forgiveness connected?

5. What did you learn from this chapter, and how can you apply it to your life?

6. What areas do you need to pray about or improve in your walk with Jesus?

Chapter 9
Ready for the Adventure Ahead

Step 1: Moral excellence is the God-given ability to perform heroic deeds.

Step 2: Knowledge is the truth of God properly comprehended and applied.

Step 3: Self-control is the restraint to trust the will of God over the will of self.

Step 4: Perseverance is the spiritual staying power that gives believers the courage to literally die instead of rejecting the faith.

Step 5: Godliness is a reverent loyalty to the obedient pursuit of Christlikeness.

Step 6: Brotherly Kindness is the selflessness of being a living sacrifice.

Step 7: Love is the surrendered choice of dying to self so others can experience Christ.

Good work! We have taken an important passage of Scripture and pulled some important truths out of it. Let's look at our focal passage once more.

> For by these He has granted to us His precious and magnificent promises, so that by them you

may become partakers of the divine nature, having escaped the corruption that is in the world by lust. Now for this very reason also, applying all diligence, in your faith supply moral excellence, and in your moral excellence, knowledge, and in your knowledge, self-control, and in your self-control, perseverance, and in your perseverance, godliness, and in your godliness, brotherly kindness, and in your brotherly kindness, love. For if these qualities are yours and are increasing, they render you neither useless nor unfruitful in the true knowledge of our Lord Jesus Christ.
—2 Peter 1:4–8 (NASU)

For me, verse 8 is an important key in this passage, and we touched on it earlier in the book. What would make someone useless in the knowledge of our Lord Jesus Christ? Unapplied knowledge. Knowing about Jesus and personally surrendering our lives to Him are two completely different things. Jesus warned us that many have knowledge of Him but few have applied that knowledge.

Not everyone who says to Me, "Lord, Lord!" will enter the kingdom of heaven, but only the one who does the will of My Father in heaven. On that day many will say to Me, "Lord, Lord, didn't we prophesy in Your name, drive out demons in Your name, and do many miracles in Your name?" Then I will announce to them, "I never knew you! Depart from Me, you lawbreakers!"
—Matthew 7:21–23 (HCSB)

These are harsh words, but Jesus didn't want anyone to miss the truth of dying to self and finding life in Him! When we give our lives to Jesus, we are doing more than stating words; we are deciding to die to ourselves in order to find eternal life in Christ.

Let me get you to answer a few questions for me. What are some of the differences between scuba diving and snorkeling? What are reasons to scuba dive? What are reasons to snorkel? When I think through reasons for scuba diving, I think of the adventure of going deeper and exploring incredible wrecks, along with seeing amazing fish and sea life found in the deeper waters plus the off chance you have to uncover hidden treasures. In addition to all these other reasons, what drives most divers is that when you begin to feel the pressure of the atmospheres, you realize that you're entering a whole new world.

In contrast, what are some reasons why people choose to snorkel instead of scuba dive? There is no training in snorkeling; you can grab a mask and go. The time commitment is far less demanding in snorkeling, and it's less expensive. Snorkeling is also a hobby that can be done alone; you don't need a dive buddy like you do in scuba; however, the most common reason for choosing snorkeling over scuba diving is fear. People fear the pressure from going deeper and the lack of complete control you have when you know your life is in the hands of your equipment, your buddies, and your training.

The contrast between scuba diving and snorkeling is an amazing parallel to the choice people of faith have to make in their own spiritual journey. Snorkeling is safe; you can see the shore. It's always easy to get back to land, back to the world. The time commitment is small and the cost is minimal. Scuba diving is deep, filled with pressure and riddled with cost. In faith, people refuse to go deeper because of the safety experienced on the surface. Occasionally, those struggling with surrender to Christ will look like snorkelers. They can take a deep breath and swim under for a short time to get an underwater picture, but then they quickly surface and get their eyes back on the shore. Driven by the fear to avoid pressure, dependency, and the cost of going deeper, many people of faith completely miss the adventure God has planned for them.

Once a person of faith commits to go deeper, the real adventure begins. Going deeper comes with greater risk and higher cost, but rewards grow exponentially greater the deeper we go. Hopefully, you will begin to see yourself on this deeper journey. Every believer eventually discovers that Jesus is in the deep.

Snorkelers can see into the deep waters with their equipment. They can point to the treasures at the bottom, but they simply refuse to pay the price to get to them. They can see bottom, but they can just as easily look up and see the shore. Followers of Jesus must never be satisfied with just seeing Jesus; they must hunger to be with Him.

Have you ever found yourself distant from God as the result of your own actions—longing for inner peace, longing to restore the joy of your salvation, and grasping to find peace in the intimate purity of God's presence? Have you ever been there? Where you are talking more at God and experiencing less intimacy with God? Where you are walking through the motions but ultimately feeling like your walk with God is more like a business partnership than a personal relationship? I have! Times like these are more like a snorkeling trip than a scuba adventure.

I've learned one overwhelming fact as I talk with Christians about this season of faith, and it's that too many of us as Christians spend a majority of our time in the proximity of God and not in the presence of God. What's the difference? Proximity is nearness as defined by geographic location. Presence is a mutual connection of attention. Let me give you an example.

When a Franklin Graham Crusade came to our community, I was given a backstage pass to do the work I was assigned for the services. On one occasion, I was standing in the back fairly close to the dressing room that had been assigned to Franklin Graham with one purpose alone. I wanted to meet Franklin Graham. For a few minutes, I tried to act busy, but ultimately, I just stood there looking awkward. When Franklin and an army of preachers emerged from his room, we were all standing in the hall together. I was even able to shake his hand as he went by me. I was in close proximity to Franklin Graham and even met him in a passing moment, but he still has no idea who I am or that we ever met. He graciously acknowledged my existence, but our encounter never got any deeper than mere proximity.

Unlike a mere moment in passing, when you enter someone's presence, your attention is focused on them, and their attention is focused on you. There is a connection between you. In other words, presence consists of a mutual connection. When we talk about the presence of God, it begins with trying to process the truth that "God's attention is on me" and that it's our responsibility to put our attention on Him. You begin to understand the gift we've been given as Christians. A gift of such value that once you've tasted of the presence of God—once you find yourself wrapped up in it—you will begin to understand the difference between being in the proximity of God and being in the intimate presence of God.

The sad truth is how easy we give it up. Even now, in a time of private confession, can you think about times you have traded intimacy with God for the deception of this world? I can think of plenty of times I traded God's goodness for the world's depravity. Many times we can feel helpless, allowing satan's pull to be stronger than your resolve, but I want to share some truth with you- a truth every Christian needs in their spiritual arsenal. *Satan cannot take you out of God's presence. You must choose to walk away.* Satan cannot rip you out of the center of God's will. Sometimes, you and I, like Adam and Eve, follow the lies of satan and voluntarily leave the peace and power of God's presence. The harsh reality is that some of us have lived in the proximity of God for so many years that we have forgotten the joy of the presence of God. So how do we return? How do we become like Mary when Jesus entered her home in Luke 10:38–42?

Satan cannot take you out of God's presence. You must choose to walk away.

On that day, Jesus visited Mary and her sister, Martha. Martha was in the kitchen being distracted, but Mary was teachable and in the presence of the Lord. Later in Scripture (Mark 14: 3 and John 12:3), we find this same Mary at a supper with the disciples and many other people that Jesus had touched. At that dinner, Mary approached Jesus, broke open a bottle of perfume, and anointed the head of Jesus in worship. Yet as the perfume dripped off of Jesus' head, the disciples saw nothing but drops hitting the floor as they talked among themselves about the waste. Mary saw the same drops pouring off His head and hit His feet, and she immediately wiped them with her hair in a moment of intimate worship and adoration.

On that day, the room was filled with people Jesus had touched, healed, and discipled. Yet every one of them was so distracted and preoccupied with their own agendas that they missed the very presence of God. They were very proud to be in close proximity to God, proud to be classified with the people of God, and, therefore, blinded to the opportunity given to each of them to place their complete attention on the presence of God.

The presence of God is the fuel for the transformational journey deeper into the image of Christ. One of the greatest transformational pictures of this is seen through the apostle John's life. Scripture allows us to see John move through the characteristics expressed in our focal passage, a journey that shaped his understanding of the Christian life. Even before John met Jesus, he was searching for truth. In fact, the first thing we learn about John was that he and Andrew were disciples of John the Baptist before they came to follow Christ. John knew what it meant to pursue moral excellence as he studied it and lived it under the teaching of John the Baptist (John 1:35–51); however, John's moral excellence grew each day he walked with Jesus. In fact, he distinguished himself enough to walk in Jesus' inner circle, the three disciples (Peter, James, and John) that Jesus called aside from time to time for prayer and encouragement.

John's biggest step of transformation came with knowledge when the words of Jesus became real to him. For John, I believe that happened at the occasion we refer to as the Lord's Supper. At two separate times, recorded at three places in Scripture, Jesus had to break up arguments among the disciples about who would be the greatest in the kingdom of heaven. In all three discussions, John was a participant. In fact, John's own mother asked Jesus to let her sons hold positions of honor, and at the end of every discussion the disciples had about their greatness, Jesus told them that to be the greatest in the kingdom of heaven, they needed to be servants to others. John did not grasp this teaching until he saw Jesus put a towel around His waist and wash his feet. In those moments, John comprehended the truth of God and applied it to his life (Mark 9:33–37; 10:35–45; Matt 20:20–28; John 13:5–20).

John's knowledge allowed him the self-control to stand at the foot of the cross when other disciples had scattered. He might not have completely understood the theology of why Jesus had to die, but he simply trusted God's will over his own. That abiding trust drove John to continue meeting with the other disciples and not to give up (John 19:26–27; Acts 1:13–14).

After the resurrection of Jesus and the indwelling of the Holy Spirit at Pentecost, John and the other disciples were unstoppable. John and Peter demonstrated great perseverance when they stood before the Sanhedrin.

> Whether it is right in the sight of God to give heed to you rather than to God, you be the judge; for we cannot stop speaking about what we have seen and heard.
> —Acts 4:19–20 (NASU)

As John and Peter continued to preach and live out their faith, they were once again brought before the Sanhedrin, but this time, their obedient pursuit of Christ had begun to make a difference, even with some of their greatest enemies.

> But a Pharisee named Gamaliel, a teacher of the Law, respected by all the people, stood up in the Council and gave orders to put the men outside for a short

time. And he said to them, "Men of Israel, take care what you propose to do with these men. For some time ago, Theudas rose up, claiming to be somebody, and a group of about four hundred men joined up with him. But he was killed, and all who followed him were dispersed and came to nothing. After this man, Judas of Galilee rose up in the days of the census and drew away some people after him; he too perished, and all those who followed him were scattered. So in the present case, I say to you, stay away from these men and let them alone, for if this plan or action is of men, it will be overthrown; but if it is of God, you will not be able to overthrow them; or else you may even be found fighting against God."

They took his advice; and after calling the apostles in, they flogged them and ordered them not to speak in the name of Jesus, and then released them. So they went on their way from the presence of the Council, rejoicing that they had been considered worthy to suffer shame for His name. And every day, in the temple and from house to house, they kept right on teaching and preaching Jesus as the Christ.
—Acts 5:34–42 (NASU)

John demonstrated godliness, also. Next, Scripture shows John and Peter on their way to Samaria. Jews looked down on Samaritans, and for centuries, they had hoped they would all die. Pure Jews considered the Samaritans impure half-breeds, the offspring of disobedient Jews who married women of other cultures, thereby weakening God's holy race; however, when Samaritans began giving their lives to Jesus, John didn't worry about who they were. He simply went and acted in brotherly kindness. His selflessness allowed many to hear the gospel and receive the Holy Spirit.

John was being transformed into the image of Christ, so that by the time he was in his eighties and writing the gospel of John, he didn't see the Christian life as an opportunity for greatness but as a character transformation driving him to emulate the very love of God. The other Gospels were written shortly after the resurrection and contain accurate historical information as well as the teachings of Jesus, but the gospel of John was written years later and solely focused on the teachings of Christ. Here's what John emphasized:

> A new commandment I give to you, that you love one another, even as I have loved you, that you also love one another. By this all men will know that you are My disciples, if you have love for one another.
> —John 13:34–35 (NASU)

> If you love Me, you will keep My commandments.
> —John 14:15 (NASU)

> This is My commandment, that you love one another, just as I have loved you. Greater love has no one than this, that one lay down his life for his friends.
> —John 15:12–13 (NASU)

By the time he wrote 1 John, understanding and living out the love of Christ permeated that letter. John had grasped what God had intended all along to draw men unto Himself: love. When you and I are willing to pursue the Christlike characteristic of *agape* love in our lives, we are not merely checking off a step in the journey but opening the door for others to experience Christ also. *The result of a life conforming to the image of Christ is not its own happiness but the fruit of others coming to know Jesus.* Jesus is not drawing you to Himself for the purpose of growing a holy huddle but to use you in reaching an unreached and dying world with the grace of a loving God.

> I pray that you may be active in sharing your faith, so that you will have a full understanding of every good thing we have in Christ.
> —Philemon 6 (NIV)

Following our focal passage (2 Peter 1:4–8), we find further instructions for our journey to Christlikeness:

> The person who lacks these things is blind and shortsighted, and has forgotten the cleansing from his past sins. Therefore, brothers, make every effort to confirm your calling and election, because if you do these things you will never stumble. For in this way, entry into the eternal kingdom of our Lord and Savior Jesus Christ will be richly supplied to you.
> —2 Peter 1:9–11 (HCSB)

I know the idea of going deeper spiritually seems like it should be driven by big words translated out of Latin or religious traditions and titles, but God's Word has always taught us an upside-down way of thinking. Have you ever wondered why the teachings of Jesus are so different from the teachings of the world? Much of the world's wisdom can be found on bumper stickers like, "The one who dies with the most toys wins!" The world is full of wisdom moving in the complete opposite direction of wisdom we see from God. Growing deeper through character transformation prepares us for the trails and pains we face in the natural course of life.

The result of a life conforming to the image of Christ is not its own happiness but the fruit of others coming to know Jesus.

Every day we face moments of conflict, tension, and stress. These are real moments in our lives where we naturally turn to the wisdom of the world. Our very nature pushes us to either flee the situation, to run and avoid the issue, or to fight. As Americans, we love a great battle; we love to win. Something in our nature is programmed to destroy what's in front of us, and conflict simply becomes a means to destroying those who have hurt us. When we feel we've been wronged, it's very natural for us to react in anger. This is because winning at all costs is not a strange concept in our world. Society has taught us all how to fight using the weapons of the world—weapons forged by the character traits celebrated in society.

Anger seems justified when someone has wronged me. Little white lies seem justified when they help me prove a greater point. Impatience seems justified when I believe my needs are more important and should be a priority to others. Revenge seems justified when I am suffering because of someone else's actions. Intimidation seems justified when I can control weaker ones to my advantage. Negative character weapons, like the ones I've just mentioned, are mastered through selfish reactions to our wounds and are compounded by the celebration of society. Each of these characteristics are modeled daily by the world around us. Society wants us all fighting and reacting with a common set of traits reflected in the values of the world. These worldly character traits are justified by the wounds of life; however, spiritual depth doesn't react with character that can be justified by the world's standards. The character of Christ first acts and then reacts as Christ would to the situations we face in life.

No one falls into the character of Christ, we must intentionally and with all diligence pursue the spiritual depth of character transformation. Over time, followers of Christ can find themselves satisfied acting like Christ but not becoming transformed into the character of Christ. Actions are only the first step to character transformation. Imagine yourself walking towards a door, and it quickly opens from the other side and jams your toes. You, reacting like the world, scream and quickly begin to curse the other person. After a few minutes you realize that your reaction had not reflected the character of Christ, so you go and seek forgiveness. You ultimately act like you should, but your reaction was still of the world. Spiritual maturity moved you to know how you should act and convicted you to go back and do the right thing. Yet, the spiritual depth of character transformation moves us past the point of needing to come back to do the right thing and moves us to a place where our reactions reflect the character of Christ. True transformation is moving us to react as Christ would react. Going back and doing the right thing is a great first step in spiritual maturity, but our goal is to react in the moment as Christ would react. Before we think about what we should do, we simply *are* the right thing because we've been transformed into the image of Christ.

The journey deeper is a life built from the choices we make in the pursuit of the image of Christ. Character transformation is the deepest spiritual journey we can undertake. I know acting and reacting like Christ isn't natural. It goes against everything we see in the world around us. It would make more sense to build spiritual depth around mysterious religious information, but the teachings of Jesus have always seemed upside down to the world.

In Christ, we have been given a new nature. Our new nature is not an external show of religious deeds displayed to satisfy our conscience but a true internal work equipped to handle life with a new set of weapons.

> I say then, walk by the Spirit and you will not carry out the desire of the flesh. For the flesh desires what is against the Spirit, and the Spirit desires what is against the flesh; these are opposed to each other, so that you don't do what you want.
> —Galatians 5:16–17 (HCSB)

Our flesh and the Spirit are at war with each other—a war carried out in the battles between the old nature I had before I came to Christ and new nature I now have in Christ. Our old nature desires to handle life one way, but the new nature calls us to handle life in a completely different manner. The wisdom of the world is seen in the works of the flesh.

> Now the works of the flesh are obvious: sexual immorality, moral impurity, promiscuity, idolatry, sorcery, hatreds, strife, jealousy, outbursts of anger, selfish ambitions, dissensions, factions, envy, drunkenness, carousing, and anything similar, about

> which I tell you in advance—as I told you before—
> that those who practice such things will not inherit
> the kingdom of God.
> —Galatians 5:19–21 (HCSB)

Some of these works come so naturally to us that we don't even think about the damage they'll leave in their aftermath. When we need to fight the battles in our lives, we naturally want to turn to the weapons of the world. Someone hurt me, so I'll turn up the anger and hurt them. I was lied to, so I'll join in and begin lying about them. We love the power of the world's weapons, so we use them.

Jesus, however, has given us a completely different set of weapons to use.

> But the fruit of the Spirit is love, joy, peace, patience,
> kindness, goodness, faith, gentleness, self-control.
> Against such things there is no law.
> —Galatians 5:22–26 (HCSB)

Those don't sound like weapons! Love, kindness, gentleness? They all sound like weaknesses: "God cannot truly intend for us to face the world using Christ-like character. The world will eat us up!" Our entire journey has been about an upside-down way of thinking. All our spiritual lives, we've heard, "Get the biblical knowledge and live a fairly moral life, and that's the key to a deep spiritual life." Yet we've learned that moral excellence and knowledge are the first two steps in this journey, not the last two. Kindness and love are the deepest steps in this journey and not some optional idea based on whether or not they fit our personalities, like we've been led to believe. It's time we put away the weapons of the world and prepare ourselves for life's battles using the weapons of God. Character transformation is the key to fighting and winning life's battles.

The Challenge

I hope and pray that you will take the time to pray through each of these characteristics and find yourself somewhere on this journey.

"Going deeper" is such a cliché in churches today. People are always talking about going deeper in their faith, but learning bigger words and fresh perspectives of timeless lessons is not necessarily what it means to go deeper. I have contended in this book that "going deeper" has more to do with character transformation than religious information. Remember what I said at the very beginning of the book. *If the church never learned another new piece of truth about God but focused on living out what it already knew to be true, we'd see unquenchable revival.*

Pray, read, serve, worship, and allow God to take you deeper into His character. It is a journey worth taking!

Study Questions

Intro video for group study can be found at
www.myjourneydeeper.com

1. What impresses you most from the focal passage 2 Peter 1:4–8?

2. What similarities do you see between the scuba/snorkeling comparison and the decisions we make pursuing the image of Christ?

3. What does it feel like to be in the proximity of God but not in His presence?

4. Is there strength in knowing the truth that Satan can't take you out of the center of God's will and that you must surrender that position?

5. If the church never learned another new piece of truth about God but focused on living out what it already knew to be true, we'd see unquenchable revival. What would it take for you to see this happen in your life, in your home, and in your church?

6. What did you learn from this chapter, and how can you apply it to your life?

7. What areas do you need to pray about or improve in your walk with Jesus?

Appendix A
The Gospel

Creation

God created a perfect world.

> "In the beginning God created the heavens and the earth."
> (Genesis 1:1 NIV)

> "God saw all that He had made, and it was very good."
> (Genesis 1:31 NIV)

In other words, God created us all for something greater.

> "For I know the plans I have for you," declares the Lord, "plans to prosper you and not to harm you, plans to give you hope and a future. Then you will call upon me and come and pray to me, and I will listen to you. You will seek me and find me when you seek me with all your heart.
> —Jeremiah 29:11–13 (NIV)

> "So you will be My people, and I will be your God."
> (Jeremiah 30:22 NIV)

> "I have come that they may have life, and have it to the full."
> (John 10:10 NIV)

God created us to be in a personal ongoing relationship with Him. God created a world without death and sin.

Human Response

Human response was sin that separated us from God.

> "For all have sinned and fall short of the glory of God." (Romans 3:23 NIV)

God created a perfect world and placed man at the center of the world, but man wanted to be like God and chose to rebel against the plan of God bringing sin and death into the world. Throughout the course of history, however, we have begun to believe that most of us are good people. We become upset when we start to think about being labeled as bad.

The truth is that we are worse than bad; we are separated from a holy and loving God.

> As it is written: "There is no one righteous, not even one; there is no one who understands, no one who seeks God. All have turned away, they have together become worthless; there is no one who does good, not even one."
> —Romans 3:10–12 (NIV)

> "For the wages of sin is death, but the gift of God is eternal life in Christ Jesus our Lord." (Romans 6:23 NIV)

But God loved us so much that he did not abandon us to the consequences of our own actions!

Return

We can return to God's plan through Jesus. God loved us too much to leave us separated from Him; therefore, He came to earth in the form of a man called Jesus, who lived a perfect life and died a sacrificial death to restore the relationship between God and man.

> "But God demonstrates his own love for us in this: While we were still sinners, Christ died for us."
> (Romans 5:8 NIV)

> "For what I received I passed on to you as of first importance: that Christ died for our sins according to the Scriptures, that he was buried, that he was raised on the third day according to the Scriptures."
> (1 Corinthians 15:3–4 NIV)

Man has created "man ways" to connect with God, but God has only made one way for Him to connect with man. Throughout history, man has tried to create ways to build or repair the relationships with God; however, at the same time, God has continued to speak about the only way for God and man to reconnect.

> Jesus answered, "I am the way and the truth and the life. No one comes to the Father except through me."
> (John 14:6 NIV)

Invites

Jesus invites you into a personal relationship with Him.

> "Yet to all who received him, to those who believed in his name, he gave the right to become children of God."
> (John 1:12 NIV)

The invitation Jesus offers is back into a right relationship with God. He is offering a new birth into a living hope. We need to always remember that our actions lead to death, but Jesus wants to pay the price for us. The cross represents God pouring out His love for us through the love and sacrifice of Jesus.

> In reply Jesus declared, "I tell you the truth, no one can see the kingdom of God unless he is born again." (John 3:3 NIV)

> "Therefore if anyone is in Christ, he is a new creation; the old has gone, the new has come!" (2 Corinthians 5:17 NIV)

Dead to the old self. Death of the old self precedes our new life.

You can't live two lives at the same time!

Salvation Is Our Gift

Salvation through Jesus is a gift He is offering to you right now. You cannot earn your salvation.

> "For it is by grace you have been saved, through faith—and this not from yourselves, it is the gift of God—not by works, so that no one can boast." (Ephesians 2:8–9 NIV)

Jesus offers salvation to you and you must decide: is your life your own, or will you give it to Jesus and allow Him to save you?

> That if you confess with your mouth, "Jesus is Lord," and believe in your heart that God raised him from the dead, you will be saved. For it is with your heart that you believe and are justified, and it is with your mouth that you confess and are saved.
> —Romans 10:9–10 (NIV)

The gift of salvation is one God has for you right now. You do not have to go somewhere and clean up your life before you come to

Jesus. He wants you right where you are and will love you into His image.

Trust

Trust Jesus to direct your life. Salvation is not the finish line of faith but the starting point of your relationship with Jesus. Once we give our lives to Him, He begins to guide us through His Word and our prayers, through the indwelling of the Holy Spirit.

> As the Scripture says, "Anyone who trusts in him will never be put to shame."
> (Romans 10:11 NIV)

Trust is an essential ingredient to a life in Jesus. It allows Jesus to transform us according to His will into His image.

> "And he died for all, that those who live should no longer live for themselves but for him who died for them and was raised again."
> (2 Corinthians 5:15 NIV)

Do you understand that sin separates us from God?

Do you believe this has happened in your life?

Do you accept what Jesus did for you?

Are you ready to surrender your life to Jesus?

Dear Jesus, thank You for loving me enough to die and bring me into a relationship with You. I want to give my life to You. Forgive me of my sins. I turn from my sin and place my trust in You. I confess You as my Lord and accept Your gift of eternal life. Transform me into Your image. Thank You for my new life! Amen.

CPSIA information can be obtained at www.ICGtesting.com
Printed in the USA
LVOW08s0847080315

429636LV00003B/9/P